TIME MANAGEMENT
FOR
CHRISTIAN WOMEN

TIME MANAGEMENT

FOR

CHRISTIAN WOMEN

HELEN YOUNG and BILLIE SILVEY

Illustrated by Joyce Stacy McMillion

PYRANEE
BOOKS

Zondervan Publishing House
Grand Rapids, Michigan

Time Management for Christian Women
Copyright © 1990 by Helen Young and Billie Silvey

This is a Pyranee Book
Published by the Zondervan Publishing House
1415 Lake Drive, S.E., Grand Rapids, Michigan 49506

Library of Congress Cataloging-in-Publication Data

Young, Helen, 1918-
   Time management for Christian women / Helen Young and Billie
Silvey.
      p.   cm.
   ISBN 0-310-51851-2
   1. Time management—Religious aspects—Christianity. 2. Women—
Religious life. I. Silvey, Billie. II. Title.
BV4598.5.Y68   1990
640'.43—dc20   89–48734
                                                                  CIP

Printed in the United States of America

Illustrated by Joyce Stacy McMillion

90 91 92 93 94 95 / AF / 10 9 8 7 6 5 4 3 2 1

To
Norvel and Frank
who have taught us to value
the precious present

CONTENTS

PREFACE

As Barbara Walters put it, "Women must balance their time more than men because they don't have wives." And what a balancing act it is, with family, job, home, church, and friends all demanding, and deserving, our attention. Most of us satisfy the external demands. Babies must be fed, reports must be written, telephones must be answered. Generally, it's those less pressing needs—deeper communion with God, rest and quiet, intellectual stimulation, physical fitness—that are neglected. After all, they'll always be there!

Despite technological advances that promised to save time, today's women are busier than ever. And they're often less satisfied. Well-educated, financially successful, appreciated at home, and respected by their coworkers, they feel hurried and empty, resentful of spending all their time handling routine duties and emergencies.

The authors are themselves wives, mothers, working women, and church women and have talked with hundreds of other women across the nation. They recognize a woman's spiritual, intellectual, emotional, physical, social, and aesthetic needs. They appreciate her desire to contribute to the broader world while maintaining intimacy with those closest to her—without neglecting the daily duties.

Time Management for Christian Women combines a firm philosophical base in God's Word, a personalized approach to help each woman adapt it to her own unique nature and situation, and a strong practical approach to getting done what has to be done and making time for more important concerns.

Much of the information for this book was collected from speeches, from church bulletins, and from discussions with Christian women over the years. If we have inadvertently failed to credit some idea or concept, please accept our apology and our gratitude.

1
My Time— What Is It?

*"My times are in
your hands."
—Psalm 31:15*

I wake up out of a deep sleep. The phone is ringing. As I grab
my robe, I stumble toward the phone.

"Hi. This is Jack Garnett from Fort Worth," a pleasant voice
drawls. "I had a message to call you." I glance at the clock. It is 6
A.M. Another writer has forgotten that we start the day later out
here in California. I collect my thoughts, grab the proper file
folder, and try to sound professional. After all, this is the
editorial office of *20th Century Christian* magazine, not just our
bedroom, and I'm an editor, not just a sleepy wife and mother
with breakfast to cook and lunches to pack.

It's typical of my days—put clothes in washer, edit copy for
magazine, call a few writers whose articles are late, eat lunch,
draft opening of a new book, pick up cleaning and the kids from
school, answer phone calls and mail, finish Bible class lesson,
start dinner, and hurry off to teach class.

The schedule varies, but it's always crowded. I feel like the
white rabbit in *Alice in Wonderland*, constantly scurrying
around shouting, "I'm late! I'm late!" If only I had more time.

I'm sure you empathize. Your schedule is crowded, too. It's
like the young couple whose combined income was substantial
but who had incurred a mountain of debts. When they were
urged to go to a financial management firm to learn how to
budget and live within their income, they replied, "We don't
need money management. We just need more money." You

may feel the same way about your time. You don't need a time management study. You just need more time.

But there is no more time. I have all the time there is—fresh every morning from God's hand to mine. Time is one area in which true equality exists. Others may have more beauty, brains, or buying power, but everyone has the same amount of time—twenty-four hours a day. No one receives more. No one receives less.

Yet we all know people who seem to accomplish twice as much as we do. What is their secret? The way they use their time, discipline their efforts, and employ their abilities makes all the difference.

Time is an urgent concern of women in general and working mothers in particular. As Barbara Walters put it, "Women must balance their time more than men because they don't have wives."

By the time I spend some of my precious hours on work, some on family and friends, some on physical fitness, some on intellectual growth, and some on spiritual development, my calendar is crammed, I am exhausted, and my time is gone. I can't get it all done. The way I think about time has a lot to do with how happy and productive I am. When I see time as insufficient, I feel hurried and harried, frustrated and ineffectual. I can't do my best work or be my best self.

An Integrated Approach to Time Management

The answer is not so much advice as an example. In Jesus we see time management at its best. He was the master of time. In three short years, he accomplished so much that history is divided by the letters B.C. (before Christ) and A.D. (after Christ). He healed the sick, forgave the sinful, raised the dead, and taught the greatest truths the world has ever known. He had time for children, widows, and the rejected. He went to weddings and dinners. Yet he spent hours—sometimes all night—communing with his Father. When we see this master of time, we cry, "Teach us to number our days aright, that we may gain a heart of wisdom" (Ps. 90:12).

But even Jesus didn't do it all. He left thousands unhealed, unfed, and untaught when he returned to the Father. Still he could say, "It is finished." He didn't do everything, but he did exactly what God wanted him to do.

Jesus had an integrated approach to time. He was neither irresponsible nor a slave to the clock. He moved calmly through the events of a short but full life, at peace with God's will and with his own nature.

We won't get it all done, either. No one can. But we can have the same integration in our lives that Jesus had, if we recognize that God gives us what we need to do the job he has for us to do. We always have time for what's essential. The key is to sift out the essential from the myriad demands each day brings.

Time Is Now

What is time? It is hours, days, weeks, months, years—calendar time. It is limitless and eternal—God's time. And it is just this instant. Now is all the time we really have—the present moment with all its possibilities.

Many women waste the present by living in the past or in the future. Corrie lives alone, consumed by bitterness over a slight she received at church fifteen years ago. "I wouldn't go back and associate with those people for anything," she says, and she doesn't. She thinks she's getting even, but she's really destroying her present by replaying her hurt past.

Ann is more progressive. She's always looking ahead. "I'll start helping teach a Bible class when my kids are out of school," she says. She's forgotten that, not so many years ago, it was "when they're out of diapers," then "when they start kindergarten." Ann plans, but she never does anything.

God is a God of the present. "I am" he called himself. The ancient Greeks' most common word for time was *chronos*, a measured period. Scripture speaks more often of *kairos*, or the moment—the fulfillment of God's perfect timing. We say that Esther was queen of Persia for a specific period of time (*chronos*), but God had brought her into the kingdom at the right time (*kairos*) to save her people (Est. 4:14).

Kairos was a minor Greek god, represented by a young man with wings on his feet and hair only on the front of his head. He represents opportunity, which must be seized as it comes, for as soon as it passes, there is nothing to grasp. That is why the sacred writers urge us to "be instant," "watch," be prepared to seize our opportunities.

The past is irretrievably gone and the future doesn't yet exist. But how many of us waste the precious present living in regret over the past or in anticipation of the future?

Time Is a Progression

Many of the world's major religions conceive of time as a cycle with no beginning or end. Reincarnation and repetition continue until some perfect state, such as Nirvana or Brahman, is achieved. Nothing new ever occurs in such a system. God can't operate, and progress is impossible.

The New Age movement has borrowed from these Eastern religions, teaching that we are reincarnated repeatedly until we reach an awareness of our godhood.

Christians reject such cyclical views of life. Instead, we confirm with Scripture that time is linear. Time began with an act of God (Gen. 1:1). Later, God intervened in time by his

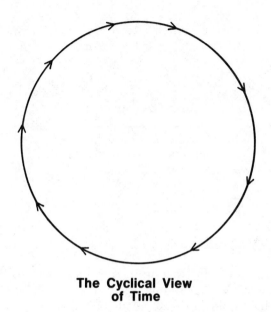

**The Cyclical View
of Time**

beginning ⟶ ⟶ ⟶ ⟶ end

**The Christian's View
of Time**

saving grace (Gal. 4:4–5). And eventually, God will bring time to an end (2 Peter 3:10).

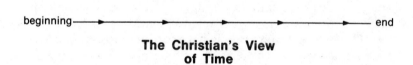

History's Timeline

When a Christian woman looks at time, she sees it as linear—with a beginning and an eventual end, as is true of her life.

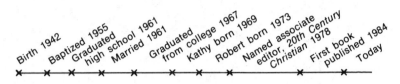

My Personal Timeline

Time Is Measured

The aspect of time that affects our lives most insistently is measured time. Measured time began with God in creation. He separated light from darkness, creating night and day (Gen. 1:3–5). He created the sun, moon, and stars to mark seasons, days, and years (1:14). And the seven days of Creation, including the Sabbath, or rest day, are reflected in our current week.

Throughout history people have tried to measure time. But for thousands of years precision in time measurement seemed less important than it does to us today. In agrarian societies days began at sunrise and ended at sunset.

A maid to Hatshepsut, queen of Egypt around 1500 B.C., depended on the sun to measure time. The shadow on a sundial, assuming that the day was sunny, was her only clock. Her calendar was based on the short solar year. Thus, an annual event which was once held in spring would gradually shift into winter.

Things didn't change much from the standpoint of telling time for the next fifteen hundred years. A woman in New Testament times could use her Roman water clock, which measured the dripping of water into a basin, even at night or on cloudy days. But since the Romans insisted that day and night were each twelve hours long, the length of an hour varied. Her Julian calendar, introduced by the emperor Julius Caesar, was still not a precise measurement of the solar cycle, and by that time it had gained ten days.

After another fifteen hundred years, Pope Gregory XIII raised the calendar to its present consistent form. A cook at the castle could be sure that Whitsuntide would fall in the same season each year. Unlike Hatshepsut's maid she could time the baking of a loaf of bread even on a cloudy day, but she had to remember to turn her hourglass over when the sand ran out, and the marks on it weren't always accurate.

Others in the Middle Ages felt the need for more precise methods of timekeeping. The monks at the nearby monastery wanted to observe scrupulous hours of prayer, so they invented the first mechanical clock for measuring hours, achieving what Daniel Boorstin calls "man's declaration of independence from the sun, new proof of his mastery over himself and his surroundings."

Master or Slave?

With the invention of the pendulum in the seventeenth century, time could be broken into minutes and seconds. As clocks became more accurate and people more punctual, we became slaves of our own devices.

Now time can be measured in nanoseconds, or billionths of a second, and the pace of our lives has increased proportionately. We suffer from what *Time* magazine has called a "time famine," and our gains in efficiency may be at the expense of other values. According to Jeremy Rifkin, president of the Foundation on Economic Trends, alienation is one result of our emphasis on speed. "The humanity is sapped out of the process because there is no room for experiencing, for savoring, or for just being."

Cecilia lives in the fast lane. She's just been promoted to the vice presidency of a major corporation. She has three children and is active in the church. She's a whiz at organization, yet sometimes she feels that life is a blur. She has to put in quite a bit of overtime, and she's missing connections with her family. Last week she made an error which cost the firm an important client. She's begun to have headaches, and life isn't as much fun as it used to be.

Time constraints cause us to make mistakes which actually slow us down. They lead to stress-induced ailments, such as heart trouble, strokes, ulcers, and migraines. And they cause us to get so wrapped up in the urgent that we neglect the things— and people—we value.

To work easily, joyously, and effectively, we need to learn to work with the Spirit as well as with the clock. Jesus said, "My yoke is easy and my burden is light" (Matt. 11:30). As his Spirit moves in us, we can work more swiftly and smoothly. Working with God, we do our best.

Time Is Relative

Although we have grown more precise in our measurement of time, there is still a sense in which time is relative. It varies by individual, by age, by activity and by culture.

Remember how long it used to take for Christmas to come? Now it seems to slip up on us. And what about the difference between an hour under the dentist's drill and an hour with a best friend? People who have been brought back from the brink of death often recall their entire lives flashing before them in an instant.

Sherry is a new mother. As she plays with her baby, she can scarcely believe how big he is. The tiny baby stage is gone forever. Looking back, she realizes that the nine months she was pregnant seemed to creep, while these first nine months with the new baby have flown—and she never gets anything done.

Time flies when you're having fun—and it moves pretty fast when you're working on an absorbing project. J.B. Priestley has pointed out that "as soon as we make full use of our faculties, commit ourselves heart and soul to anything, live richly and intensely instead of merely existing, our inner-time spends our ration of clock-time as a drunk sailor his pay."

God didn't make us to run on the strict time schedules we've adopted. Our biological clocks don't tick at the same speed our mechanical ones do. Women, in particular, have bodies that operate on a lunar cycle, even though our clocks and calendars are based on the sun. Most adults have biological clocks of sixty-three minute hours, so they lose a day almost every month. That's why we function better at different hours of the day and different days of the month and why we're sometimes "out of sync" with the rest of the world.

The pace of life varies from region to region in this country and from culture to culture throughout the world. According to a study by Robert Levine, Japanese people move faster and have even more accurate clocks than most Americans or Europeans. Italians and Indonesians move slower, and their clocks are set less precisely. To keep someone waiting is frowned upon in our culture, but in Southern Europe and Latin America, flexible schedules are assumed.

Our emphasis on speed creates problems in a rapidly shrinking world. Businesswomen, missionaries, and other travelers must adapt to the varied pace of different societies, and all of us need to learn that our concept of time is not the only one.

I learned my lesson at a wedding shower for our Spanish preacher's son and his bride-to-be. Arriving at the fellowship hall a few minutes before the invitation specified, I found the groom's mother, Carmen, still wearing her housedress, preparing food. I helped her with the work, urging her to go change before the other guests arrived. She worked on calmly until the job was done, then changed clothes and returned before anybody else got there.

We can learn from more relaxed, slower-paced cultures. Brazilian sociologist Vianna Moog has pointed out that "the American no longer knows how to contemplate; he does not know how to reflect or even rest."

A child of missionaries to Africa returned to the U.S. to find that "everything seemed to blare out; do, taste, experience, buy, absorb, read, feel, be—and *quick*, before it's too late."

Time Is Change

Our faster pace of life means an increased rate of change. In contrast with the Egyptian, Roman, and medieval women who lived in agrarian cultures where change was the exception, some of us have experienced the development of the airplane, television, space travel, and home computers within our own lifetimes. Change occurs so rapidly that we struggle to keep up.

When I was a child, I worked with my father in his newspaper office. By the time I graduated from high school, my skills—operating a linotype machine, hand-setting type, and running a letterpress—were all outmoded. Everything was done by photo offset. I had to learn a new trade.

The law of entropy states that the universe itself is winding down. As we grow older, we become painfully aware that our bodies decay. But Christianity stands above time, claiming permanence in the midst of flux. "Therefore we do not lose heart. Though outwardly we are wasting away, yet inwardly we are being renewed day by day" (2 Cor. 4:16).

As Christians we can continue to grow spiritually long after our bodies have reached their physical peaks. We can use our time to grow toward perfection.

Time Is a Gift

Time is a precious gift of God. In C.S. Lewis's *Screwtape Letters*, the experienced demon counsels his nephew to tempt people to believe that their time is their own. Screwtape knows, however, that "man can neither make, nor retain, one moment of time; it all comes to him by pure gift; he might as well regard the sun and moon as his chattels."

We speak of killing time, but time is life, and to kill it is to commit slow suicide. Because time is such a precious gift, we must not squander it. We should use it wisely to God's glory.

When God spoke from the burning bush, he asked what Moses had in his hand.

"A rod," Moses answered.

God told him to throw it down, and it became a serpent. When Moses picked it up, it became a rod again. With that rod Moses led the Israelites from Egyptian bondage, divided the sea to save them, and provided water to sustain them.

Our time is like that rod. When God asks, "What is in your hand? What do you have available for my work?" we answer, "Minutes, hours, days—time!"

"Cast it down," God says. "Spend yourself in love and service." When we do that, God transforms our time, which is intrinsically neither good nor bad, into a great display of his power.

There may be risks involved. The risk of picking up a serpent must have given Moses pause. But it was nothing compared with challenging one of the most powerful rulers of that day. Moses offered his resources, and God used them mightily.

"What is in your hand?" God asks us. We have his gift of time, and he challenges us to do great things with it. But he reminds us that it's not what's in our hands, but the fact that we're in his hands, that makes the difference. R.H. Grenville makes this clear:

Time

What is Time?
    A ticking clock,
A hurried call,
    An urgent knock?
Tasks to do
    By such-and-such?
A tyrant who
    Demands too much?

Time is NOW,
    The vital, true
Experience of being you.

Take your time.
    Relax and be
Aware of all
    Eternity,
For time is not
    The pressure-pace,
The calendar,
    The daily race
To beat the clock;
    Not stress and strife.
Time is what we do with life.

Questions and Activities

1. Read the book of Mark, giving special attention to Jesus' use of time.

2. How can we recognize "God's moment" in our lives?

3. Make your own personal time line, starting with your birth and including special events in your life. Imagine the present as a continuing spot, moving on the line.

My Personal Timeline

4. How has your concept of time changed since you were a child?

5. Imagine yourself living in an earlier, agrarian age. What would be more difficult about life then? What might be simpler?

2
My Mission
and My Goals

*"Mary has chosen
what is better."
—Luke 10:42*

When my husband Norvel became president of Pepperdine University, our four children ranged in age from three to twelve. I was editing *Power for Today*, trying to relieve Norvel of as much detail work as possible, and teaching a Bible class at the Vermont Avenue Church and a college course on marriage and the family.

We entertained often, opening our home to prospective faculty members, the board, and other campus groups. At the same time, I was trying to start the Associated Women for Pepperdine, a support group to raise money for scholarships.

Realizing that Pepperdine needed to make friends in the community, I became a member of Freedoms Foundation, the Muses of the Museum of Science and Industry, and the women's division of the Los Angeles Chamber of Commerce.

Gradually I came to realize that I was neglecting the children. I had arranged for the best schools I could find and for carpools to take them there, but taking care of the children was my responsibility. No one else could do that for me.

So I started taking them to school instead of having someone else drive them, stopping to talk with their teachers, and letting Norvel go to the basketball games at Pepperdine while I attended their programs at their school.

I made a point of taking them with me, one at a time—even to the grocery store—just to be with them. We let them stand with us in the receiving line at receptions and began sharing our concerns at the dinner table.

My problem was one of choices. I had to determine the best use of my time and find ways to do what I considered important.

Planning My Destination

Can you imagine taking a trip without knowing where you are going in advance? You wouldn't know whether to pack your swimsuit or your ski outfit. You might fill the tank with gas and the car with children and luggage and snacks, but if you just took the nearest road out of town, where would you be?

When we plan a trip, the destination is our first decision. Knowing makes all the difference in how we prepare and the route we take. So it is with our lives, our time. It's easy to spend twenty or thirty busy years, then awaken to realize that we are getting nowhere.

Most women who have trouble with time management don't need help learning how to do more. We are already over-committed. We need to learn to be more selective about what we do. We need to learn to make wise choices, to center our lives on those things which are most important, and to make better use of our time.

But before we begin tracing the route to our destination, let's see where we are now. The following questions may help:

1. Do you often feel confused and scattered?
2. Does there seem to be too much to do and not enough time to do it?
3. Do you get satisfaction from your work?
4. Do you enjoy your family and friends?
5. Do you take time for a daily appointment with God?
6. Do you have time to rest, eat, and exercise?
7. Do you spend most of your time on things which are important to you, or on things which just have to get done?
8. Do you look forward to some time in the future when it will all come together?
9. Do you have any idea what you'll be doing in five years?
10. When you die, what would you like your obituary to say?

Our answers to these questions can help us evaluate where we are now.

Releasing the Beauty

Just as a sculptor, standing before a block of stone, glimpses a statue inside it, so we all have dreams of the finished form we want our lives to take. We can envision what we want to be like and what we hope to accomplish.

Our job is basically the same as the sculptor's—to remove the extraneous, releasing the potential beauty from the mass surrounding it. A less experienced hand might remove too much, gouge into a vital area, and spoil the dream. But the sculptor, with infinite care, removes only the nonessentials.

What do you want to be when you grow up? When you're a

finished work? *Perfect*, or mature, is the word the Bible uses (Matt. 5:48), though none of us is ever thoroughly mature.

As Christians, our basic pattern has been given by God in the example of Jesus. We are to be like him. "For we are God's workmanship, created in Christ Jesus to do good works, which God prepared in advance for us to do" (Eph. 2:10).

We can call this final, idealized form of our lives, our ministry or mission. Our mission is determined by three interrelated factors: God's will for us, our individual nature and gifts, and the circumstances of our lives.

Discerning God's Will

As Christian women, we have many demands on our time— home, job, relationships, worship, community service. But these demands may have little to do with God's will for us. Pat King, a mother of ten, has learned that doing God's will does not mean meeting all expectations. "Instead, it means discerning in my heart what I've been called to do and saying no to what I haven't been called to do."

The Scriptures teach a similar lesson. We are not to be anxious about the physical demands of life, but to "seek first his kingdom and his righteousness" (Matt. 6:33). Paul talks of the "one thing" which he does (Phil. 3:13–14). He tells us to make "the most of every opportunity" . . . and to "understand what the Lord's will is" (Eph. 5:16–17. See also Col. 4:5).

The philosopher Søren Kierkegaard in his *Purity of Heart Is to Will One Thing* explains it this way:

> The person who in decisiveness wills to be and to remain loyal to the Good, can find time for all possible things. No, he cannot do that. But neither does he need to do that, for he wills only one thing, and just on that account he will not have to do all possible things, and so he finds ample time for the Good.

Prayer plays an important part in discerning God's will. We remain close to him through regular devotional periods and by assembling with his people for fellowship and praise. As much as we understand it and are able, we do his will, depending on his grace and forgiveness when we fall short. We trustingly affirm with the psalmist, "My times are in your hands" (Ps. 31:15).

Several years ago, I discovered that I was often too busy to spend time meditating on God's Word, praying, and listening for his direction. I determined to turn things around. For me, that meant getting out my Bible and spending a few quiet moments with God before my day began—no matter how busy I was. I still have occasional lapses, but I have discovered that the time I spend with God is not time away from my other tasks. It is time that gives me the perspective and power to meet the demands of life.

The time I spend with God helps me make those decisions which center my life on my mission. It helps me avoid the frantic busyness which plagues our world today. It gives me the strength and confidence to meet life calmly. And it lays a firm foundation which improves the quality of my life and helps make me a better person.

Discovering My Nature and Gifts

The Bible speaks of a fleshly nature which is at war with the spirit. But there is another nature which should be at perfect peace with God's will. It's the distinctive nature God has given each of us. This nature is easy to understand when we look at the apostle Paul. Paul was headstrong, determined, and zealous—both as an opponent of Christianity and later as a Christian missionary. That was Paul's nature, and God used it mightily.

You may be totally different. You may be timid and shy and sensitive to the feelings of others. You may be a leader or a follower, spontaneous or well organized, intellectual or emotional. As Anne Ortlund said in in her *Disciplines of the Beautiful Woman*, "Every woman has some nebulous thing" which makes her "choose what she chooses. It influences whether she marries or doesn't; gets a job or not; whether she's messy or elegant, too fat, zealously intellectual, sexy, overcautious, organized, deeply spiritual, full of fears—you name it. Something guides us all inside."

You can discover your nature by taking a personality profile test. But the simplest way is to list those things you enjoy doing, the experiences you've had which demanded your best and brought satisfaction, what others say about you, and those personality traits which make you tend toward one or the other of such opposites as society versus solitude, physical work versus mental work, teaching versus doing, challenge versus security.

Whatever your nature, there's a place just for you in God's scheme of things. Don't try to mimic someone else. Be the best *you* you can possibly be.

God also gives us special gifts that he expects us to exercise in his service. The Bible lists such gifts as serving, teaching, encouraging, exhorting, leading, giving, showing mercy, and having wisdom, faith, and spiritual discernment. (See Romans 12:6–8, 1 Corinthians 12:8–11, Ephesians 4:11–13, and 1 Peter 4:10–11.)

Are your gifts in this list? Do you have other gifts? The answer to at least one of these questions should be yes, because each of us is gifted. Pray that God will help you identify your gifts and use them for him.

Considering My Circumstances

Your mission will also vary according to your circumstances. Are you single or married? Do you have five children or none? Are you a student, homemaker, working woman, or combination?

Mary Dean Lee has studied four main circumstances, which she calls life-space structures: home-based nuclear (focused on the home), work-based nuclear (focused on a job), conjoint (focused equally on job and home), and diffuse (focused outside of both home and job).

She found that different people derived varying degrees of satisfaction in each of these situations based on the degrees of choice, excitement, and interaction they offered.

Our life-space structure is determined by family, finances, education and job availability—but it is also influenced by our values. What is important to you? A higher income? Job fulfillment? Being at home when the kids get out of school?

Michelle, a single woman, is a gourmet cook. She finds

great satisfaction in entertaining friends at home, while Nancy, who hates to stay at home, gets her greatest pleasure from her art classes at the community college. Although both are single career women, Michelle has a home-centered structure, while Nancy's is diffuse.

Life-Space Structures

Home-Based Nuclear (focused on home)	Life centered primarily around family and homemaking
Work-Based Nuclear (focused on job)	Life centered primarily around office or career
Conjoint (focused equally on both)	Life centered on work during work hours and home the rest of the time
Diffuse (focused on neither)	Life centered on some interest outside of either home or work

Problems arise when you fail to consider your circumstances in determining your ministry or mission. Several years ago, a young wife and mother wanted to start a class for babies in the church. She put a great deal of time and effort into purchasing high chairs and other materials for the class. Her husband felt she was neglecting their home and their own baby. But she was so determined to serve God in that particular way that she left her husband for a man who agreed with her values. If only she had waited until her situation changed. As the baby got older, she would have had more time for outside activities.

God doesn't want us to wreck our families. The people who depend on us are his special gifts. We only have them for a short time. Ask a widow or a mother whose children have recently left home how important—and how brief—this time with our families can be.

Women's circumstances change often in the course of a lifetime. Look at your life as an evolving whole. If you aren't married now, you may be later. If you have children at home now, you won't for long. If you have a job skill, it soon may be outmoded. John Naisbitt, in *Megatrends*, says that "the notion of lifelong learning is already replacing the short-term approach to

education, whereby you went to school, graduated, and that was that." He points out the need for generalists. "If you specialize too much you may become obsolete."

When you have studied and prayed for God to reveal his will for you and have considered your own nature, gifts, and circumstances, you should have some concept of your mission or ministry. Don't feel intimidated by the words or chained to your conclusion. This is the basic thrust your life should take at the present time. It will change as your understanding evolves, your circumstances change, and your walk with God grows closer.

The Good, the Bad, and the Ultimate

Just about the time you have a clear picture of your current ministry, the cat will knock over a vase of flowers, the spaghetti will boil over on the stove, or the plumbing will back up. None of these things is remotely connected to your mission in life, but they have to be dealt with. They are the sorts of emergencies which can crowd out the important things in our lives.

Often more demands are made on us than we have the resources to meet. So many good causes beckon that we easily become overextended. We can be very busy and accomplish little of value. We must remember our mission and learn to say no. There are only so many things we can do well. Joyce Brothers has pointed out that "it's better—as well as easier on you—to devote yourself to one job and do it well than to dabble in several with the guilty feeling that you're really not giving your best to any of them."

We tend to think of the choices we make as choices between good and bad. Hard work is good; laziness is bad. Sharing is good; hoarding is bad. A clean house is good; a mess is bad. But there's a third category which should enter into our thinking. Among good things, some are better than others. Even among bad things, some are always bad, while others may be good in certain situations.

Jesus' visit to the home of Mary and Martha (Luke 10:38–42) demonstrates this principle.

Martha was a practical woman, and she knew when she was being taken advantage of. She was doing all the work of serving, while her sister sat at Jesus' feet. Martha demanded justice. She got a lesson we all need.

"Martha, Martha," Jesus said, "you are worried and upset about many things, but only one thing is needed. Mary has chosen what is better, and it will not be taken away from her."

Like most of us, Martha had a scattered mind. She was "worried and upset about many things." The things on her mind weren't bad. They were good. But only one thing was ultimate, and Mary chose it by listening to Jesus.

Many of our basic values are just as obvious:

1. God first

God is our Maker and Sustainer. He is the center of all that we are and do. He will accept no other priority. When we seek him first and strain toward his upward call, we are making the most of our time.

Not that we deal with God and then go on to our next priority. God should permeate our entire lives. As Gordon

MacDonald says, "The inner world of the spirit must govern the outer world of activity." We should live in light of our eternal aspirations. Most of the things we do are good, many are urgent, but few have ultimate significance.

2. People second

When we put God first in our lives, everything else falls into perspective: "Love the Lord your God with all your heart and with all your soul and with all your mind . . . and . . . love your neighbor as yourself" (Matt. 22:37–39). In other words, when God is first, people are second.

Naisbitt points out that increased technology leads to an increased need for the human touch. "The more technology we introduce into society, the more people will want to be with other people," he says. "We must learn to balance the material wonders of technology with human spiritual demands."

It's easy to become occupied with things that need to be done and see people as interruptions. But God teaches us to value people, love them, and seek their good. Life is a constant series of choices based on such values. The kitchen floor may need waxing, but when your son comes in bruised and bloody after falling out of a tree, the floor can wait.

Concern for others does not come automatically. It must be cultivated. We are essentially selfish, and it takes thought and effort to treat others as we want to be treated (Matt. 7:12), to look out for their interests as we would our own (Phil. 2:4). But that is God's challenge to each of us.

After God, our top priority should be our physical family. The wife of a noted theologian threw his manuscripts into the fire upon his death because he'd neglected his family to write them. We should care for our husbands, our children, our ailing parents, but not pamper them to the point that they fail to develop unselfish Christian love.

We also love our extended families, our spiritual families, our friends, strangers—all who need our help. Jesus taught in his parable of the Good Samaritan (Luke 10:29–37) that our neighbor is anyone who needs us.

3. *Things third*

That puts things last, not that we can neglect our responsibilities. We have houses to clean, reports to prepare, clothes to
keep up, meetings to attend, meals to cook, projects to
complete, and errands to run. But as urgent as these things are,
they cannot take the place of God or people in our lives.

Our consumer society encourages dissatisfaction with what
we have and places an unrealistic value on material things.
Some women find their greatest joy in shopping. But the volume
of things which confront us when we step into a store can
consume time which might be spent more effectively. We can
now choose from 530 models of cars and trucks. One store in
New York stocks 2,500 different light bulbs! How long would it
take to find just the right one?

It is idolatrous to become inordinately preoccupied with
things and spend more time and money on them than we do on
people and on God. If we evaluate our needs, curb our
appetites, and simplify our lives, we will free time for things of
ultimate value.

Early in my marriage I decided my priorities would run like
this: God first, Norvel second, the children third, the church and
its calls fourth, and Christian education fifth. As I look back over
the years, I find my priorities are still the same, except that I
have added grandchildren to third place!

Setting Goals

Once you have established your mission and lined up your
values, you are ready to set some specific, long-term goals.
Where would you like to be in five years—in terms of your
spiritual, personal, family, professional/financial, and your so-
cial/community life?

These long-term goals should be clearly defined and a
realistic deadline set for their completion. For example, I want
to have the first draft of this book finished by September, or I
want to have my kitchen organized before I begin my holiday
baking.

Goals are ends you can take responsibility for yourself,

without someone else's help. For example, you can make it your goal to be a better wife, but not to have a good marriage; to see that your children do their homework, but not to have them make all A's; to pursue accounts with five new firms, but not to have a certain volume of sales. Your goal can be to lose twenty pounds, to research your family history, or to save fifteen dollars on groceries each week.

My Ministry or Mission

To love God with all my heart, soul, and mind; to love others—especially my family—as myself; and to serve others through a ministry of writing, teaching, and encouraging.

My Long-Term Goals

1. *To develop a closer relationship with Christ*
   to strengthen my commitment to daily devotions
   to worship God more fully
   to read some of the classic devotional books

2. *To have a closer relationship with Frank now that the children are growing up*
   to spend more time together
   to think of thoughtful little things to do
   to go out together, just the two of us

3. *To rear productive Christians*
   to spend more time with each of the kids
   to encourage their Christian growth
   to get them both through college

4. *To grow in my professional abilities*
   to give more creative thought to the magazine
   to finish three new books
   to read books on writing

5. *To deepen friendships*
   to write or call friends across the country
   to invite at least one person or couple to dinner per month
   to send cards and call local people who are sick, shut in, or bereaved
   to reach out to strangers—especially those in need

Your goals should be consistent with your mission. If they aren't, then either your goals or your mission should be restated. And remember that your goals change as you and your circumstances change.

Each long-term goal should be divided into a series of short-term goals, or steps toward meeting it. For example, I'll draft a

chapter every other week, or I'll shop for shelf paper and drawer dividers this week, clean out one section of cupboards next week, etc.

Of course, not everything you do will advance your goals. Far from it. But you can do a little each day toward meeting at least one of them.

Your overall mission or ministry, your long-term goals, and your short-term goals form a framework, a rough sketch of the way you'd like your life to come out. Then, like the sculptor, you can give your imagination free rein to flesh it out as you desire, dealing calmly with the emergencies that arise, spending time with God and the people who need you, glancing from time to time at the sketch to keep you on course, and revising it as your circumstances change or your understanding of God's will grows.

According to Ortlund,

Under that wonderful umbrella of "if God wills," we need to see what provisions are necessary for each leg of the journey and get them. Then we need to say no, no, no daily to everything that would get us off course, and keep returning and returning to our personal charts to make sure we're getting there.

Then we will truly have all the time we need. As Michael Quoist put it:

Lord, I have time.
　　I have plenty of time.
All the time that you give me,
　　The years of my life,
The days of my years,
　　The hours of my days,
They are all mine.
　　Mine to fill, quietly, calmly,
But to fill completely, up to the brim,
　　To offer them to you, that of their insipid water
You may make a rich wine
　　Made once in Cana of Galilee.

Questions and Activities

1. Spend five to fifteen minutes a day this week in devotion to God and in prayer that you'll come to know his will for you.

2. Discover your nature and gifts by taking a personality profile test or answering these questions:

What do you enjoy doing?

What experiences have demanded your best?

What experiences have brought the most satisfaction for you?

What do others say you do well?

Which do you prefer? Society or solitude? Physical or mental work? Teaching or doing? Challenge or security?

3. According to Mary Dean Lee's study, what is your life-space structure? Has it ever changed? Do you expect it to change again?

My Ministry or Mission

My Long-Term Goals

4. Are you more like Mary or Martha? In what ways?

5. At the top of this page, or on a separate piece of paper, write your mission or ministry as you understand it at present. Then list five long-term goals—in such areas as your spiritual, personal, family, professional/financial, and social/community life. Leave space between them to list several short-term goals and steps for meeting each one.

3
My Daily Plan

*"Making the most
of the time ... "*
—Ephesians 5:15–16 RSV

Soon after Christmas vacation I begin to hear it: "I can't wait for summer to come." All through the spring the chorus swells. Before long, I'm looking forward to it, too. Those lazy days of summer. Afternoons on the beach. Picnics in the park. Finally, the long-awaited day arrives. Yearbooks are signed, report cards are picked up, and the kids come home to three glorious months of sleeping late, visiting friends, watching TV, reading, and loafing. But before many days have passed, I hear that other plaintive cry associated with summer: "I don't have anything to do." Then I know it's time to start listing activities, planning outings, and assigning extra chores.

If you're like me, it's been a long time since you've complained of having nothing to do. I'm much more likely to be overwhelmed by the number and variety of tasks at hand than by the dearth of activities to fill my time.

One day recently, I finished an article for *Pacific Church News*, edited copy for *20th Century Christian*, went by the Social Security office to get a card for my sixteen-year-old, and prepared a lesson for my Bible class. The next day, I got out seventy letters for the Ethnic Evangelism Seminar, had lunch with a friend, worked on a book I'm writing, got groceries for the week, and kept a doctor's appointment.

As Horatius Bonar wrote in *God's Way to Holiness*, "If we would aim at a holy and useful life let us learn to redeem time. There need not be routine but must be regularity, not mechanical stiffness but there must be order. There may not be haste, but there must be no trifling with our time or that of others."

When Paul speaks of redeeming, or making the best use of time, he is referring to our opportunities. The idea isn't to crowd more into the day, but to be alert to opportunities to communicate the message of Christ—both in words and in lifestyle.

Redeem means to buy up or buy out. It is like a housewife shopping for an item she knows will be on sale only once. She buys the entire stock, knowing she won't be able to get it again at such a bargain. In a similar way, we buy out our time, using it as productively as possible, knowing that it is all we have and that we will never again be at this particular point in our lives.

Productive use of our time does not mean that each minute's activities lead to some concrete end. Some things we do—watching a sunset, listening to a child or older person, relaxing, reading a good book, visiting with a friend—are ends in themselves.

Five Keys to Jesus' Use of Time

Jesus understood the principle well. His life was far different from our lives today. And, while most of us wouldn't want to live in a world without cars or electricity or indoor plumbing, we want to be like him. What was Jesus' life like? How did he use his time? What can we learn from his example?

Tom Olbricht, in *The Power to Be*, says, "Great men [and women] are always busy. Jesus was no exception. He had a mission, a goal for his life. There was much to accomplish and only a few years to complete it."

Mark's account of Jesus' life repeatedly uses the word *straightway*, or *immediately*. Jesus no sooner finished one task or activity than he began another. Despite tremendous pressure, however, he never seemed frantic or rushed. He moved swiftly but calmly from one event of his full life to the next.

According to Olbricht, "Jesus did not keep an appointment book in his tunic. His life, however, was a series of successive appointments—he simply turned the appointment book over to someone else." With his life under God's control, he was able to fulfill his goals and still withdraw often to replenish his resources.

Here are five keys to Jesus' use of time:

1. Direction

Jesus could use his time to the greatest advantage because he knew what he was here for. "My food . . . is to do the will of him who sent me and to finish his work" (John 4:34).

2. Prayer

Jesus knew the power of prayer. The Gospels record seventeen instances of his praying. Once he woke up before daybreak and went out to a lonely place to pray. Another time he prayed all night.

3. Single-mindedness

Jesus was compassionate and responsive to people's needs, but he did not allow himself to be swayed by their demands or debilitated by guilt over those things he didn't get done.

4. Individual Attention

Jesus dealt with individuals one at a time. He spent a great deal of time talking to a sinful woman by a well. As he was on his way to heal a sick girl, a woman reached out to him. He stopped to heal her, then proceeded to raise the girl, who had died in the meantime.

5. Hard Work

Jesus was not afraid of hard work. One day early in his ministry, he taught in the synagogue, cast out a demon, went home with Peter and healed his mother-in-law, and then healed and cast out demons from a crowd which had gathered once the news spread. "As long as it is day, we must do the work of him who sent me. Night is coming, when no one can work" (John 9:4).

In addition to these principles from Jesus' life, there are other practical principles which can help us make the most of our opportunities.

Write It Down

Most of us have so many things to do, we run the risk of forgetting something urgent or being so paralyzed by the demands on our time that we have trouble doing anything. As William James said, "There is no more miserable person than one in whom nothing is habitual but indecision."

The first day of orientation in college, the professor asked, "How do you tell a freshman from a senior?" We just looked at each other, so he answered his own question, "When you walk into a classroom and say, 'Good morning,' the freshmen say, 'Good morning,' but the seniors write it down."

I started right then to write things down. First it was class notes, then grocery lists, then lists of things to do. Now I'm an inveterate list-maker. Lists help. The best cure for indecision is a clear plan. The greatest need for good time management is to know what to do next.

I live by lists. I love checking off the things I have done, but every day there are items left over that must go on tomorrow's list. There is rarely a day when I check off everything on my list. I have often said that the day I die I will still have many things on my list of things "to do." But I'm sure those things left undone will be his will for someone else.

The Importance of Planning

Did you know that God has a plan for you? " 'For I know the plans I have for you,' declares the Lord, 'plans to prosper you and not to harm you, plans to give you hope and a future' " (Jer. 29:11).

An unfortunate translation in the King James Version has given many women a problem in this area. In the Sermon on the Mount, Jesus is quoted as saying, "Take no thought for the morrow." I have a relative who canceled his insurance policy when he read that verse. Actually, in the original Greek, Jesus' words were not "Take no thought," but "Have no anxiety." He was not teaching against planning, for he taught the importance of realistic plans in the story of the man who wanted to build a tower but failed to estimate the cost and was unable to finish it (Luke 14:28).

Instead, Jesus was teaching us not to worry. He emphasized that repeatedly in Matthew 5. Good planning will help us avoid anxiety. We can actually have better mental health, for misman-agement of time puts us under pressure and fills us with guilt.

But we need to beware of buying into time management ideas without running them through the Bible filter. For one thing, we may become too consumed with means and not give enough attention to ends. William T. McConnell, in *The Gift of Time*, says that some Christians have applied the world's managerial principles to housekeeping, with books for home-makers which sound like Heloise's hints with quiet time added.

We should seek to know God's will and to make it basic to the way we manage our time. All our time belongs to him, and when we see it as a gift rather than a resource, we want to use it in harmony with his wishes.

Letting him direct us, we launch out in faith. As James Neuman put it in *Release Your Brakes*, "Adventure is the deliberate volitional movement out of the comfort zone." Most truly worthwhile work is outside our comfort zones, involving risk of failure. Loving other people may be the greatest risk of all.

One of the joys of my life is to feel that I have accomplished something worthwhile that is within God's plan for me. Sometimes I can almost hear him say, "Well done," when I check off an item on my to-do list. I have more energy, both physical and mental, for the next task. I am relieved of the pressure of a half-finished job and the guilt of procrastination.

Planning gives me time to enjoy life, for I feel that I am in control, not that circumstances are controlling me. My life is less complicated, and I find myself making progress toward my goals. Since I plan time for spiritual growth and for being with family and friends, I know the joy of pleasing God and making life more enjoyable for others.

One executive estimates that every hour of planning saves three to four hours later. When Winthrop Rockefeller was governor of Arkansas, he spent one hour each evening planning his schedule for the next day. With a well-thought-out plan, he was able to complete his most important tasks in a regular working day. He could then go home and concentrate on his family.

It's great to get organized. It takes discipline, but it also can be fun. It's good to plan, especially when we work our plan "as ever in our great taskmaster's eyes," as the poet John Milton said. God is a God of order, and he challenges us to do all things "in a fitting and orderly way" (1 Cor. 14:40). One of the best ways to be orderly is to use an organizer.

Choosing My Organizer

Some women resist using an organizer because they fear it will limit their spontaneity. Just the opposite is true. Using an organizer gives reassurance that you've covered the essentials. Then you can feel free to take off, knowing that you haven't forgotten anything important. (If my husband and I had had an organizer as a young couple and had written the correct address in it, we would not have gone to the wrong wedding reception.

We did have a good time, but we wondered why we knew so few of the people there!)

Others feel they don't have time to plan. Perhaps you are too busy feeding the baby to write in or read an organizer if you had one. But if you find yourself hunting a scrap of paper with a telephone number on it, or losing the grocery list in your own purse, or needing a telephone number when you are away from home or an address when you are at the post office, then an organizer will simplify, not complicate, your life. It will save you time, because you will not be looking for things or missing appointments. Using an organizer frees time by reducing the waste of uncertainty and limiting each day's load to what is most important for that day.

Organizers come in many sizes and formats. Check a stationery store for one that fills your needs, or make one by setting up the forms you want and copying the pages. Your organizer should reflect your own lifestyle. Still, commercial products can suggest ideas for your modification.

You will probably want one which includes an appointment calendar—monthly, weekly, or daily, depending on the number of appointments you generally have on a given day; a to-do list for jotting down things you'd like to accomplish; a project planner for working out the details of larger projects; and a goals section to list your long- and short-term goals.

You may also want a section for financial records, including due dates for bills or notes, the children's allowance, and your giving plan for the church and for missions or benevolence.

Some organizers have sections for addresses and phone numbers (including birthdays and anniversaries); Bible study and sermon notes; records of calls to make, letters to write and people to entertain; prayer lists, shopping lists, and gift and size lists.

My organizer includes a list of the lessons in each unit of the Bible class I teach. It allows me to look ahead and plan the lessons and the bulletin boards for each unit while I'm waiting at the garage or doctor's office. I also keep a record of the letters I write and the books I read each year.

Anything you need to have with you when you're away from home should be in your organizer. Anything you want close at hand when you're at home should be there, too.

Using My Organizer

As with any tool, an organizer must be used to be helpful. You should write in it whenever you make an appointment or think of some task to do. And you need to refer to it throughout the day, marking off appointments and tasks as they are completed and adding any new activities that come up.

The following plan may help you use your organizer:

1. Long-Term Planning

Block out events on your monthly calendar as far in advance as possible so you can look ahead and work on things before they're due. This is known as the art of the early start, and it automatically builds in a stretch factor to allow for glitches in the project or unrelated emergencies.

For example, once when I was scheduled to speak for a ladies' class in a neighboring city, I became quite ill a week

Monday, May 22

Appointments	To Do
8	
9	
10	
11	
12	
1	
2	
3	
4	
5	
6	
7	
8	

Notes (or Expenses)

before the class met and wasn't able to work on my lesson for several days. Fortunately, I'd started preparing early, and the lesson was almost complete.

Long-term planning allows you to practice backward scheduling, backing up from the deadline for a project to a date which gives you time to finish it with ease. Try to start a few days earlier than necessary to allow for emergencies. Then break the project down into separate steps, and do a little each day or so until it's completed.

Students can use this system by sitting down with the syllabus from each class and listing reading assignments and papers due in their organizer. Then schedule backward to finish each project well in advance.

When I took a college course recently, I felt almost smug as I turned in paper after paper early, while my fellow students stayed up all night the night before the due date. Of course, I'd done the same thing at their age, but as I grow older, I don't have the energy for "all-nighters"—or maybe I now have the organizational skills to avoid them.

Long-term planning allows you to keep control of your schedule. Elton Trueblood marks off large blocks of time to study, write, and be with his family. Then, when he is asked to do something which he considers a lesser priority, he says, "I am sorry, but my schedule is already full for that time."

Young families will want to block off time for family nights and birthdays, anniversaries and special times. You will want to put down the children's ball games and school plays and appointments of other family members who require coordination.

Refer often to your goals and priorities. They will cause you to say no to many things, to eliminate some, and delegate others. But they will make your life more unified and help you accomplish more of the things you consider important.

2. Planning Your Week's Activities

Set aside time once a week to rough out the next week's schedule. I try to work on my schedule on Friday evening, listing all appointments and tasks which must be done on certain days.

Many are already in my organizer, but I check to be sure there isn't a note in my purse or by the phone which hasn't been included. This is the time for consolidation.

Aunt Isabel from Maine had a rigid weekly schedule. She washed on Monday, ironed on Tuesday, mended on Wednesday, cleaned on Thursday, and baked on Friday. I, too, have projects that I've assigned to certain days: a play on Mondays, the time book on Wednesdays, and my novel on Fridays.

I have lists of routine items—for job and home—which I schedule on certain days of the week. For example, I read bulletins and iron on Monday, read and clip magazines and journals on Tuesday, cull files and mend on Wednesday, file and work on notebooks on Thursday, and catch up correspondence on Friday. When I have extra time, or just want to sit down with a cup of coffee, I pick up one of the routine projects for that day.

3. Keeping a Daily Appointment with God

Ideally we need not separate our devotions from our day, but can relate our time with God to all our plans and activities. If we will integrate our quiet time into our plans for the day, we can live in the context of God's will.

Martin Luther once said, "I have so much to do today, I must pray an extra hour." He explained his devotional habits in a letter to his barber in 1535. Titled "A Simple Way To Pray, for a Good Friend," it is a beautiful example of integrating a quiet time into all the day's activities.

Luther began by reading the Bible and praying. He used a notebook so his thoughts on the Scripture would not be forgotten. "The weakest ink is more enduring than the strongest memory," he said.

Luther suggested four questions to make your study more practical: (1) "What am I grateful for?" What in the text causes me to be thankful? (2) "What do I regret, or what makes me sad?" From this Scripture reading, what prompts me to confess my sins? (3) "Whom should I pray for in addition to myself?" Family, friends, the sick, those in crisis, the poor, the world in need. And (4) "What am I to do?" As James says, "Do not merely listen to the word. . . . Do what it says" (1:22).

This last question relates to our "to-do" list for the day. Adding the activities we discover in our devotional time to our list of things to do will help us live out God's will from day to day.

Suggestions for Planning

1. List appointments, activities, deadlines, and social events as they come up on a monthly calendar. Transfer them each month to your daily organizer pages.
2. Add time for daily devotions.
3. Add daily activities and errands.
4. Add steps toward goals and long-term projects.
5. Add time for family members, friends, and others who need your help.
6. Allow time for yourself—meals, rest, grooming, etc.
7. Add any other activities which result from your daily devotions.
8. Prioritize your list.

We will want to pray for things that are not related to our Scripture reading for the day. We will want to do things which are not suggested by the Scripture. We can do that by asking the same questions with a broader application.

Tying our devotional period to our day helps us know what to do next. It helps us know what not to do. And it helps unify our lives. As we pray about each item and write it in our organizer, we will see how it relates to our Christian commitment.

When we seek God in planning our day, we will not allow the urgent to crowd out the important. We will sift our priorities and eliminate the unnecessary and the unproductive. We will find a new sense of freedom and joy, and we will have more time for ministering to those in need.

Our quiet time may be ours alone, or we may share it with our spouse, coworker, friend or other family member. God will bring a new unity of purpose as you seek his will together.

The staff of *20th Century Christian* in Nashville begins each day with a devotion. Everyone is there, from the publisher to the man who sweeps the floor. They read *Power for Today* together and ask God's blessings on their work. These few minutes in the morning give them a sense of unity and energize them for the day.

I start each day with an appointment with God. After pouring a second cup of decaf, I sit down with my Bible, my organizer, and the daily newspaper. I allow at least half an hour (the newspaper can go) and not more than an hour for devotion, planning, and keeping abreast.

I ask God's direction as I add items from my to-do list, a step from some long-term project, one or two items to help advance my goals, and one or two routine tasks. If something comes to mind, I jot it down. If I can't work it in today, I figure out when I can and put it on the calendar. "The Lord will fulfill his purpose for me," the psalmist says (138:8).

Living in Los Angeles, I have to figure driving time into my appointment scheduling. I try to give myself at least a ten-minute cushion to allow for heavy traffic. Thus, I plan to leave thirty minutes early for a meeting twenty minutes away, or an hour early for a luncheon forty-five minutes away.

I have call sheets and address pages in my organizer, so I list the calls I need to make—work, church and personal—while I'm planning. My friend Marla, who produces a radio program and makes numerous calls each day, keeps a running list of phone calls on her computer. Each morning, she updates the list and prints out a copy.

4. Prioritizing Tasks

Once you've made up your daily list, the next step is to prioritize. A good way to determine your number-one priority is to ask yourself: "If I could do only one task today, what would it be?" If it has to be done, do it first. Then, even if an emergency throws the rest of your schedule awry, you will have worked on your most important task.

Most time management systems suggest using a 1, 2, 3 or an A, B, C system to prioritize the entire list. One (or A) tasks are high-priority items which must be done that day. Two (or B) tasks have later deadlines, but should be completed as soon as possible. Three (or C) tasks can be put off.

Many of the tasks we know we can do well are C's, while A's

often involve the risk of doing something new. We may be tempted to say, "I'll get these C's out of the way, then I can concentrate on the A's." That's an excuse and a waste of time.

It has been estimated that eighty percent of the value of the things we do comes from twenty percent of our activities. In other words, in a list of ten items, two will be A's, representing most of the value of the entire list. Do A's first, then B's.

Some C's are trivial and will just disappear if you wait long enough. Others, if deferred, will become A's or B's. Organizing files or recipes are C's; they only become A's or B's when they start costing time because you can't find things.

If you only have fifteen minutes before you need to leave for an appointment or start dinner, start an A rather than doing a C. As Mary Abrams pointed out, "The magic word is Start." Jot down some notes, an outline, a list. It will get your juices flowing, and the job will be easier to finish when you return.

Some A's are long-term projects—learning a language, writing a book, restoring an old house. They demand a regular investment of time. Just fifteen minutes a day adds up to nearly a hundred hours in a year. That's two and a half working weeks!

5. Working Your Plan

The best schedule in the world is useless unless it is implemented. Paul admonished the church at Corinth: "It is best for you now to complete what a year ago you began not only to do but to desire, so that your readiness in desiring it may be matched by your completing it out of what you have" (2 Cor. 8:10–11 RSV).

Carrying out your plan demands: (1) Motivation. Let God give you the strength, "for God is at work in you, both to will and to work for his good pleasure" (Phil. 2:13 RSV). (2) Discipline. Self-control comes from his indwelling Spirit (Gal. 5:22–23). (3) Sensitivity. Remain sensitive to God's leading and to the needs of others. Japan's famous Bullet Train was designed to zip along on a single track, ignoring all else, but Christian women were not. (4) Peace. Don't allow a heavy schedule to keep you from experiencing God's peace.

Be realistic. Pace yourself. If you have odd moments on

your hands, check your projects or goals for something to start on. If you're too pushed, move a few items to a later date. Adjust your schedule to accommodate only those things you can handle comfortably. Each day has its own tolerance level, and you only frustrate yourself if you try to crowd too much in.

Don't be discouraged if you finish the day with items remaining on your list; most of us do. Focus on what you've been able to accomplish. Don't look at leftovers as failures. Simply reschedule them on a later, slacker date and forget about them until then. As Betty Glass points out, "Some days there is no point in trying to finish anything but the day itself."

Timesaving Tips

1. If your organizer is too large to carry easily, keep a small notebook and calendar in your purse to jot down appointments and ideas when you're away from home. Don't forget to consolidate at least once a week—more often if you find yourself letting things slip.

2. Don't bite off more than you can chew. We tell our children when they are small, "Don't take such big bites." Let's take our own advice. "Just say no" to tasks which overextend you. Know your limitations and capabilities. I usually try to get about half a dozen things done a day. A man who lectures on time management says he does ten, but either he does less time-consuming jobs or he works faster. If you have a new baby or a health problem, you may do well to do one or two. Try it a few days and adjust to what you can handle without undue stress.

3. Tackle a dreaded task first. If you dread calling to apologize to someone, ask a favor, or decline an invitation, do it first. We encourage our children to eat their brussels sprouts first. When I eat cake, I save the icing for last. This is the way I like to manage my time. I do the hard or distasteful first and get it out of the way. Then I can reward myself with more pleasant tasks. I hate to figure my expense account, so I work on it first thing in the morning. I'm so glad to have it done that it makes the whole day brighter. And I'm constantly surprised to find that it usually doesn't take as long as I feared.

4. Use your best time (the time when your energy is highest

and you're most alert) for the most important or difficult tasks. Don't waste it on activities like telephoning, which can be done when energy is at a low point. Some tasks require concentration and should be grouped in times when you're less likely to be disturbed. Others, like yard work, must allow for weather and time of day. A high-protein snack—a few spoonfuls of cottage cheese or a handful of nuts—can give you the energy boost you need to get through a meeting at a "low" time.

5. Focus on one thing at a time. My friend Betty tells me that cashiers at the bank don't look at all the people lined up in front of their window; they concentrate on one customer at a time. Otherwise, the tellers would be overwhelmed, they would get tense, and service would suffer. If you have prioritized your list and prayed about it, you can be confident that the task is important enough to demand your full attention. Don't worry about what you're not getting done. Do this one thing well.

6. Plan for variety. I like to put my dishes in to soak, then start on a writing or editing project. By the time my mind gets tired, my body needs the change and the dishes have almost washed themselves.

7. Stop when your work becomes unproductive—when you get tired or start making too many mistakes. A good mental attitude and a sense of accomplishment stimulate energy, but frustration drains it.

8. Begin a task even if you know you won't have time to finish it. It will be easier to pick up the next day, and your subconscious can be working on it in the meantime.

Your daily plan is a means to an end—your end. Let it be your servant—not your master. Be flexible and open to God's interruptions, those serendipities God sprinkles along our paths. To treat your organizer like a taskmaster standing over you with a whip is just another way to forfeit control of your time—and the joy of productive time management.

A good program of time management can diminish the need for remembering details. It regulates the flow of work by allowing you to divide jobs into bite-sized chunks and spread them over several days or weeks. It enables you to anticipate and defuse potential work overloads. It helps you tailor your time use to your own goals and values. And it allows you to approach life in calm serenity—knowing that your time is under your control as you are under God's.

> Drop thy still dews of quietness
>   Till all our strivings cease.
> Take from our minds the strain and stress,
>   And let our ordered lives confess
> The beauty of thy peace.
>
> *John Greenleaf Whittier*

Questions and Activities

1. Which of the five keys to Jesus' use of time do you need to incorporate or emphasize—direction, prayer, single-mindedness, individual attention, hard work? Choose one and work on it during the coming week.
2. Do you have an organizer? If not, shop for one, thinking through the features you need. If you already have one, study the way you use it to see if you could be more effective.
3. Look ahead to events or deadlines and try backward scheduling to allow plenty of time for preparation.
4. Incorporate some of Martin Luther's suggestions into your daily devotions.
5. If you haven't already done so, make a to-do list for today, adding thoughts which came to you in your devotions.

4
Past, Present, and Future

"Encourage one another daily, as long as it is called Today."
—Hebrews 3:13

I admire the aliveness of people who give themselves to the present moment and to the people who are with them at that moment. It is an act of love to give yourself in full attention and concern to the people in your lives.

My husband, Norvel, is better at this than anyone I know. Every morning he wakes up and says, "Isn't it a great day to be alive?" It may be sunny or foggy. It may be 5 A.M. But he keeps me constantly aware of how precious each day is.

We put on our jogging suits and go down to the track, and he says the same thing to all the people we meet there: "It's a great day to be alive!"

He gives people the sense that he has time for them. He is totally present for them, not thinking of something else he needs to do, or the next appointment, or the last one.

People—each one is of significance to God. The waitress in the restaurant (Norvel knows her name, how many children she has, where she is from), the checker in the grocery store, all the simple day-by-day transactions with people can be "thirty-second islands" of caring when we treat each one as God's children instead of just a casual contact.

When I think of the people who influenced my life as a child, I think of those who got down on my level, asked me questions, and listened carefully to what I had to say.

New Every Morning

Let's focus our attention on the immediate events of the present moment, the now. It is the only real time there is or ever has been in which to live and act. It's so easy either to live under the specter of the past or under the pressing need to get ready for the future that we miss the present.

Christianity is a religion of new beginnings. It starts with the new birth through baptism (John 3:3, 5) and continues as we are raised with Christ to "live a new life" (Rom. 6:4), constantly purified by Jesus' blood (1 John 1:7).

Time is like the manna that God gave the children of Israel in the wilderness. It came for that day only. They could gather it, and they could eat it to sustain their lives. But if they tried to hoard the manna, it spoiled. They could not get more than they could use for one day.

It's the same with time. We have twenty-four golden hours, 1,440 diamond minutes. They are God's precious gift to us. We should treasure them more than money. We spend a lot of time thinking about how to save a dollar while we waste our minutes, the priceless currency of life.

Each day is new and represents a new opportunity. The psalmist tells us that "weeping may remain for a night, but rejoicing comes in the morning" (30:5). And Jeremiah reminds us that

> The steadfast love of the Lord never ceases,
>   his mercies never come to an end;
> they are new every morning.
>   —Lamentations 3:22–23 RSV

Yet, as Mark Rutherford wrote in *Deliverance*, "If we were to reckon up all the moments that we really enjoy for their own sake, how few should we find them to be." We often live like the colony of space travelers in this science fiction story. Leaving their own doomed planet in search of a new home, they encounter on the way all the adventures that characterize life. Babies are born; people die. Many live their entire lives in transit—longing for their former home or looking forward to the home to come. They miss the joys of the trip, which is all they really have.

We are no different. The home we have left is the past— furnished with familiar surroundings and peopled with family and friends. Our new home is the future—beckoning us with the lure of adventure and the unknown. But the present, the time we have now, seems insignificant. We rush through it on our way somewhere else.

At the Mercy of Memory

It's fun to look back over our lives—to read old letters and journals, to turn through scrapbooks and photo albums, to celebrate anniversaries, birthdays, and reunions.

My sister is writing a history of our family. She has collected hundreds of old letters, and she pores over them, extracting fragments to construct chapters in the lives of some who are still living and some who died long ago. This is a legacy she is compiling for her children and grandchildren, and she is enjoying the process as she discovers more about her roots.

Memory is the mother of compassion. God repeatedly urged the Israelites to remember that they were strangers in Egypt, and thus to deal kindly with the strangers in their midst. We are to remember our sins so we won't repeat them, to remember the forgiveness God has given us so we can forgive others, to remember the help he's provided and thus know how to offer help to others. We can learn a great deal from the past, but we shouldn't be tied to it.

1. Regret

Regret is one cord that binds us to the past. We berate ourselves for our sins, mourn our lost opportunities, and are paralyzed in the present because we can't live down our past. Despite God's wonderful promise, "I will forgive their wickedness and will remember their sins no more" (Heb. 8:12), we hang onto our guilt in destructive ways.

Paul never forgot his failures. He was aware that he had been a "blasphemer and a persecutor and a violent man." But he was also aware of God's grace, which "was poured out on me abundantly, along with the faith and love that are in Christ Jesus" (1 Tim. 1:13–14).

Paul accepted the forgiveness Jesus offered. Thus he was able to forget the past and "press on toward the goal" (Phil. 3:13–14). We can, too, if we stop dwelling on our mistakes and learn from them, if we stop saying "if only" and start saying "next time."

The Holy Spirit is at work in us, helping us to grow more loving, joyful, peaceable, patient, kind, good, faithful, gentle, and self-controlled. We shouldn't chain ourselves to a defeating self-image based on mistakes of the past. Rather, let us pray for God's Spirit to work in us, smoothing our rough edges. God isn't finished with us yet.

2. Nostalgia

Another cord that can bind us to the past is nostalgia. Those carefree days of childhood, the thrilling years of youth—before the children were born, before we started going downhill—are bathed in a warm glow, like the gold light used in television commercials. People were kind then. They were honest. Everybody went to church.

But "the good old days" weren't really as good as they seem. They had their pains and disappointments. And the present isn't as bad as we believe, either. After all, today will be somebody's "good old days."

As John C. Raines wrote, "Whatever freedom means, we are not free to undo this past. The freedom comes in how we relate this past to our future. We can drown ourselves in regret, lose ourselves in nostalgia, or cling to these old injuries and losses. But if we do, it is our *choice*, not our destiny."

We can never cut off the past. It is too much a part of us. God revealed himself in history, and the record of his dealings with people in the past forms the basis of our understanding of his nature and dealings with us.

The public television series *Connections* showed how many of the technological advances we enjoy today can be traced back through a series of related discoveries. Although the connections were not immediately evident, progress in one area stimulated development in another, all the way from the simplest discovery to the most complex. In a similar way, through a strange series of births and marriages, we are influenced by the generations which came before us.

The Scriptures recognize our debt to the past: "As an example of patience in the face of suffering, take the prophets who spoke in the name of the Lord" (James 5:10). We owe a debt to those who form our religious heritage—prophets, apostles, godly men and women of the Bible. We owe a similar debt to those teachers and ministers who influenced us on a personal basis. "Remember your leaders, who spoke the word of God to you. Consider the outcome of their way of life and imitate their faith" (Heb. 13:7). And we owe a debt to those who influenced us the most—our families. "Honor your father and mother" (Eph. 6:2).

Living on Borrowed Time

While some look back to the past, others look ahead to the future. They are the planners and dreamers of the world. In this book we've encouraged good planning. We recognize the value of dreams and ambitions, of postponing gratification, of investing now for future rewards.

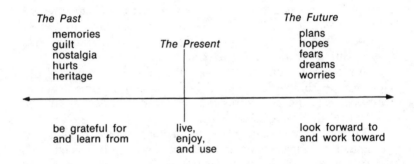

When I was a child, my parents gave me piano lessons. I was not mature enough to appreciate the value of practice, however. All I could see was how boring it was to sit inside, picking out one note after another, when the sun was bright and my friends were all having fun outside. I couldn't see ahead to the satisfaction a perfected skill could bring, so I dropped my lessons.

My son is going through something like that now. When he gets his allowance, he can't wait to find a way to spend it. Then when Christmas or someone's birthday comes around, he's upset because he has no money left to buy presents.

As Michael Le Boeuf writes, "One of the problems with instant everything is that it lulls us into neglecting the future. All that matters is the urgency of satisfying present needs."

Practicing skills, getting an education, starting a savings account, gaining experience, and organizing a project are all

ways to invest now for rewards later. There are risks, however, in concentrating too much on the future.

1. Waiting

Where some say "if only," others say "someday." Like the two men in *Waiting for Godot*, we anticipate an event which never occurs. We may wait to make more money before sharing what we have, to be wise before teaching what we know, to have ten talents before using the one talent God has given us. We may be waiting to turn twenty-one, to buy a BMW, to put our last child through college, or to pay off the mortgage. But the writer of Proverbs tells us, "Do not boast about tomorrow, for you do not know what a day may bring forth" (Prov. 27:1. See also James 4:13–16).

We may be waiting to arrive without realizing that the true

joy comes in the journey. A president of West Texas State College told of working with some friends to dig a cave. They worked hard in the heat and wind, looking forward to the fun they'd have playing in it. Looking back later, he realized that the fun was in the digging. They rarely played in the cave once it was finished.

As a writer, I know what it's like to work hard to reach that last chapter, that last word on the last page. But I've discovered that, instead of being excited, I usually feel sad when it's all over. The fun is in the writing, not in the finished product.

As Edith Schaeffer says, "People so often look with longing into a daydream future, while ignoring the importance of the present. We are all in danger of thinking, 'Someday I shall have courage to start another life which will develop all my talent,' without ever considering the very practical use of that talent today."

2. Worrying

Worrying about things that may never happen is another counterproductive way to live in the future. "No man ever sank under the burden of the day," Gordon MacDonald writes. "It is when tomorrow's burden is added . . . that the weight is more than a man can bear. . . . If you find yourself so loaded, at least remember this: it is your own doing, not God's. He begs you to leave the future to him, and mind the present."

Jesus said, "Each day has enough trouble of its own" (Matt. 6:34).

The only legitimate use of the future is to enrich the present—to chart directions to begin moving toward now. When we look ahead in this sense, we can fill spare time with constructive activities, anticipate logjams in our schedules and begin clearing them, and count the cost—in time, energy, and money—of activities we'd like to pursue (Luke 14:28–30). We can't eliminate all surprises, nor should we want to. But we can reduce the unpleasant ones which are caused by poor planning.

A stitch in time saves nine, and by being aware of those nine potential stitches—not worrying about them, but just being aware—we'll take the one stitch that makes the others unnecessary.

Just as Christianity looks back to God's work in history, it also looks forward to his victorious end of history. In light of those two lines of sight, we are called to walk by faith today. Faith, according to Mother Angelica, is having "one foot on the ground and one foot in the air, with a queasy feeling in your stomach. . . . But don't stop because you're afraid," she admonishes. "Grace comes with that one step—and you get the grace as you step."

The Sacred Now

Even as we look back to the past and forward to the future, we realize that all we really have is the present moment. We need to cherish it, relish it, and use it well, for it is a holy moment, the sacred now.

The present is a wonderful gift from God—fresh and unsullied and full of possibilities. Like a daily deposit of $86,400 made to your checking account, which must be used or lost, he gives us 86,400 precious seconds each day. We should receive his gift with gratitude and joy, make the best use of it we can, and show love to others—now.

1. Today is the day to enjoy.

Make the moment an emotional success by responding to simple things, expecting the best, liking work and people, being cheerful and decisive. "This is the day the Lord has made: let us rejoice and be glad in it" (Ps. 118:24).

Joy should be the natural state of the Christian. The word *joy* appears in the Bible more than two hundred times. Sixty-three times in the New Testament, Jesus and joy are associated. The gospel writers use the words *cheer, merry*, and *laugh* five times each; *glad*, seven times; and *rejoice*, eighteen. Yes, Jesus was a man of sorrows, but he was also a man of joy. He wants us to be happy, as he was, by being fully conscious of God's love and obedient to his will.

Norman Cousins has written of the value of joy to our

physical well-being. He has scientifically studied two groups of people with cancer. One group talks about positive things, shares funny stories, and has a confident approach to their chances for recovery. The other group receives only the standard treatment. Through his study, and through personal experience, Cousins has discovered that a joyful spirit leads to physical well-being. "He who laughs, lasts."

2. Today is the day to act.

This gift of God, the present moment, also carries a responsibility—we must use it. Someone has said that "the best time to plant a tree was twenty years ago. The second best time is now." Today is the day to say kind words, to stretch our minds, to be creative, to pray, and to listen to the prompting of God's Spirit. "I tell you, now is the time of God's favor, now is the day of salvation" (2 Cor. 6:2).

There is an urgency about the Scriptures. Pick out the verbs in the Bible—*go, repent, arise, teach, witness, seek*—so many are verbs of fervent action. Get up and get busy seems the essence of Bible teaching. And it is true. Time is short. Our life is just like the fog on our campus in the morning that by 10 A.M. is gone. It is like the steam from the tea kettle which disappears before we know it. You and I don't know if we will live through the night. We have no guarantee of tomorrow. Today is the only day we have.

We should be like the woman who heard from her doctor that she had only one year to live. Based on the things she valued, she began making decisions about her time and soon gained an appreciation of people, beauty, joy that she had never known before. Since we don't know how much time we have, we should make every bit of it count.

A couple of the students in my Bible class were frightened by rumors that the world was to end on a particular day in September 1988. When they asked me about it, my answer was similar to what Thomas Jefferson wrote his daughter over two hundred years earlier: "I hope you will have good sense enough to disregard those foolish predictions that the world is to be at an end soon. The Almighty has never made known to anybody at what time he created it; nor will he tell anybody when he will put an end to it. . . . As to preparations for that event, the best way is for you to be always prepared for it."

3. Today is the day to show love for others.

People slip out of our lives so quickly that we must help them now, while they can benefit from our ministry. Children grow up so fast, we must enjoy them now. Our parents and our husbands age and die; we must appreciate them now. In this world we pass each other so fleetingly, perhaps never to meet again. Even a smile or a kind word may do lasting good.

When Mary was criticized for anointing Jesus' feet with costly ointment, he defended her. "Let her alone," he said to her critics. "The poor you always have with you, but you do not always have me." We must take advantage of opportunities while they are available.

If you have a nine-year-old daughter, do you realize that she has already been in your home half as long as you can expect to have her there?

Today is the day for planning, but it is also the day for spontaneity. Remember the friend you had an urge to call? You found her sick and depressed, and you were able to help. Remember the weekend you suddenly decided to load up the family and get away for a while? It remains one of your most precious memories. We are told, "Do not put out the Spirit's fire" (1 Thess. 5:19). In other words, "Don't stifle a good impulse."

Big Ben, the tower clock in London, bears this inscription on its face, "If not now, when?" And we might add, "If not by me, by whom?" Don't just say, "We must get together for lunch someday." Set a definite date. Don't promise to take your children to the park or the zoo. Do it. Someday is a day which never comes.

Living in Day-Tight Compartments

Of course, we can't do everything. God doesn't expect us to. We should live our lives in bite-sized pieces. But though Jesus taught us to pray for our daily bread, most of us want a loaf in the breadbox and a couple in the freezer—just in case.

When my husband Frank was in the Navy, serving on an aircraft carrier, he took me on a tour of his ship one day. He showed me the heavy oval doors which sealed off the various compartments. They were watertight and fireproof, so that damage could be contained in one part of the ship and the rest could remain afloat.

Our days must be like that—lived in day-tight compartments. A child would be overwhelmed if we tried to give him a college education at one sitting. We give it to him one day at a time—through elementary school, junior high, high school, and college. In the same way, we don't become mature Christians in a single bound. We meet the challenge of Christian living the way the alcoholic meets the challenge of staying sober—one day at a time.

Don't let yesterday's troubles or tomorrow's worries dampen

today's joy. Don't let the magnitude of the task overcome you. As Seneca said, "Count each day a separate life."

God will give us strength to deal with the present situation. "As your days, so shall your strength be" (Deut. 33:25 RSV).

Praise be to the Lord, to God our Savior,
   who daily bears our burdens.
                                            —Psalm 68:19

As Dietrich Bonhoeffer wrote, "I believe God will give us all the power we need to resist in all times of distress. But he never gives it in advance, lest we should rely upon ourselves and not on him alone."

My friend Catherine Dye founded a fine private school, the John Thomas Dye School, in Los Angeles. She is a charming and elegant woman who has contributed to the education of thousands. Each day the children at the school recite "The Salutation to the Dawn," a little poem from the Sanskrit which is sometimes attributed to Kalidasa. It says a lot about the importance of this day:

> Listen to the Exhortation of the Dawn!
> Look to this Day!
> For it is Life, the very Life of Life.
> In its brief course lie all the
> Verities and Realities of your Existence:
>   The Bliss of Growth,
>   The Glory of Action,
>   The Splendor of Beauty,
> For Yesterday is but a Dream,
> And Tomorrow is only a Vision:
> But Today, well-lived, makes
> Every Yesterday a Dream of Happiness,
> And every Tomorrow a Vision of Hope.
> Look well therefore to this Day!
> Such is the Salutation of the Dawn!

Questions and Activities

1. What do you know about your family heritage? Have you traced your family tree? Is there anyone who could supply information?

2. Are you haunted by sins for which you haven't accepted forgiveness? Pray for God's forgiveness and praise him for your freedom from guilt.

3. Are you holding grudges? Make things right as far as possible, and then let go.

4. Are you spoiling the present by waiting for or worrying about some future event? How can you live a more satisfying and grateful life right now?

5. How would you live today if you knew it was your last day on earth? Whom would you want to show love to? Do it now.

5
Killing Time

> *"Whatever your hand
> finds to do, do it with
> all your might."*
> —*Ecclesiastes 9:10*

When I was younger, I loved to go hunting. That was back in the time when every kill was dinner for your family—before we realized that wildlife is a limited commodity and guns are dangerous to have around. I remember getting up early in the morning—long before daylight—and sitting in a cramped duck blind until my toes were numb.

I have killed only one duck in my life, but I was so proud of it. I took it home and cleaned it and made a wild rice dressing to go with it. Then our family sat down to a feast.

Even then, I considered murder an incomprehensible sin. How could anyone take the life of another human being? I could never identify with murder. Until I read Fyodor Dostoyevski's *Crime and Punishment*. Dostoyevski was such a consummate artist and his characters so convincing that I was soon proved wrong. I found myself living every moment of the spiritual awakening of the young murderer, Raskolnikov.

While I have never even been tempted to attack another human being, I am a murderer. We all are. As Benjamin Franklin said, "Dost thou love life? Then do not squander time, for that is the stuff life is made of." We all let precious time pass, like sand through our fingers, without taking advantage of the opportunities it affords.

As recovering alcoholic Barnaby Conrad wrote, "I confess to missing drinking on long flights on airplanes; it was a good way to kill time (what a dumb concept anyway; we don't kill time—time

kills us). And what sort of idiot wants time to pass quickly when that's all we truly have?"

How many people have you read about or known who, after a heart attack or other life-threatening illness, made a complete turnaround in the way they live? While we admire their new appreciation for life, they are admitting that they have not always valued it.

The fact is that all of us suffer from a life-threatening illness. We are all terminal. And we should live in light of the sobering fact that death will come—perhaps much sooner than we expect.

Not that we should fill every moment to the brim with frantic activity. It may be that we need to slow down to make better use of our time. Or, as business consultant Robert T. Riley points out, we may need to learn the difference between efficiency and effectiveness. According to Riley, efficiency is doing anything well or right, while effectiveness is doing the right thing.

There are a number of ways we can fritter away our time. Some are obviously lazy and wasteful, yet others may look surprisingly virtuous. Anything that keeps us from the fullness of life God intended for us is a sin, and should be put away with all the other sins in our lives.

Perfectionism

I like to see myself as Superwoman, today's woman, gracefully combining family and career and still managing to look smashing, maintain warm relationships, and contribute to society. It doesn't always work that way. In fact, all too often I rush around like a crazy person, looking disheveled, feeling frantic, and unable to enjoy the time and relationships I'm blessed with.

That's a hard admission to make. I expect a lot of myself, and I feel like a failure when I don't measure up. So I punish myself. Unable to be satisfied with the many things I do accomplish, I chide myself for the few I let slip. It makes me tense, dissatisfied, and not much fun to be around.

It's a matter of self-image, and I tend toward two extremes. First, I'm overconfident. After all, if I can do five things well, why not ten? On the other hand, I don't have enough confidence just to be myself—to let both my strengths and my weaknesses hang out. I try to maintain an impossible façade, and the effort is exhausting. None of us is perfect, and we shouldn't pretend to be.

Perfectionism is one of those deceptive sins which sounds almost like a virtue. After all, I try so hard. How could that be wrong?

For one thing, it shows that my values are misplaced. Some jobs demand my best, but others don't. If I put the same effort into mopping the kitchen floor that I do into writing a book, something's out of kilter. "If it's worth doing, it's worth doing well" may be my motto, but if I have eight tasks to do today, and I try to do them all perfectly, my day won't end until tomorrow. God gave me a mind, and he expects me to use it. I must decide which jobs deserve my best effort and which can be given "a lick and a promise."

Perfectionism indicates unrealistic expectations. I may have more to do than can be done in the time allowed. If I expect the possible, I won't be disappointed so often.

Perfectionism hints of rigidity. It's a problem Christians especially are prone to. We want to do things right, and once we decide what right is, we tend to do it that way forever. Jesus taught us the right way to handle a problem with our sister (go to her first), to give (cheerfully), and to lead (by serving). But he didn't tell us the right way to type a letter or wash a car.

An incident right after our marriage brought this lesson home to me. Frank and I had brought the clothes in from the line and were folding them when I glanced over and laughed. "That's not the way to fold a towel," I said.

"It isn't?"

"Of course not. Here, let me show you." And I proceeded to third the towel lengthwise, then quarter it until it made a nice, compact bundle.

When my mother, who was visiting some time later, pulled out a towel from our linen closet, she asked, "Why do you fold your towels this way?"

I was bewildered. "It's the way you taught me," I said.

"That's because I had narrow little shelves," she explained. "It was the only way towels would fit. You have plenty of room to open them up more."

Perfectionism makes us hesitant to delegate. We're afraid that, if we don't do it ourselves, it won't get done—or at least not well.

Finally, perfectionism destroys our self-esteem and makes us miserable. In his book *Getting Things Done*, Edwin C. Bliss says that the pursuit of excellence is gratifying and healthy. The pursuit of perfection is frustrating and neurotic. We can never live up to our high expectations, so we castigate ourselves and aren't very easy on those around us. "It's a terrible waste of time."

Change is not easy. We have to learn to trust ourselves and other people, but primarily we need to trust God and his unconditional love.

Seven Deadly Sins

1. Perfectionism
limit the number of tasks you try to fit into a day

accept your failings
learn what's really important
try different ways of doing things
delegate tasks
learn to trust yourself, others, and God

2. *Procrastination*

attack unpleasant tasks first
accept the possibility of failure
recognize your self-worth
tackle jobs in small bites
list advantages and disadvantages of completing jobs
set specific deadlines
let others know your plans
reward yourself for completing a task

3. *Habitual Tardiness*

leave early for all appointments
have something constructive to do if you arrive early
relax and enjoy the trip
slow down and reduce errors
take time for adequate preparation
clear your mind
don't overcrowd your day

4. *Anxiety*

value yourself
trust God
recognize the uselessness of worry
pray
work
concentrate on others
replace negative thoughts with positive ones

5. *Indecisiveness*

accept the fact that all your decisions won't be perfect
think things through
collect data
discuss the question with God, others
set a deadline
take the first step
trust your impulses
establish priorities

6. *Anger*

count to ten
avoid antagonizing others
work off anger in harmless activities

try to understand why the person did what she did
express anger calmly
distinguish between trivial and important anger

7. *Excessive Entertainment*

be aware of the time you're spending on entertainment
limit viewing time
be selective in your entertainment choices
consider alternate activities
balance work and entertainment
if all else fails, remove the TV

Procrastination

Procrastination—needlessly postponing important tasks—is another time killer. A poll quoted in an editorial in the *Los Angeles Times* indicates that the average worker wastes nine work weeks a year by procrastinating. That's almost a fifth of the year, and it costs employers more than pilfering and embezzlement put together. The procrastinator is not only killing time, he's stealing from his employer.

Psychologists say that women are more likely than men to procrastinate, and that fear of failure and distaste for tasks are the major causes.

Procrastination can make even the smallest task loom large. Pressure builds, and when work is finally begun, it is never our best. "Begin!" Horace urged. "He who postpones the hour of living right is like the rustic who waits for the river to run out before he crosses." Consider how painful procrastination is and how satisfying it feels to get a dreaded job out of the way.

As M. Scott Peck puts it, "Delaying gratification is a process of scheduling the pain and pressure of life in such a way as to enhance the pleasure by meeting and experiencing the pain first and getting it over with. It is the only decent way to live."

We may need to start with just a small bite. Daniel Schantz tells of being instructed on his first day of school to copy his full name from a cardboard name tag. "I looked at my name," he says. "Daniel Dean Schantz. Seventeen letters. Chinese, for all I knew. Despair. Tears slid down my face, and my fingers suddenly felt like big sausages." When his teacher saw his tears, she covered all the letters but the first one. "Let's make a *D*," she said. And gradually, a letter at a time, the impossible task was performed.

Time management experts advise procrastinators to spend just five minutes a day on a job they've been putting off. That's a relatively painless way to get started, and often getting started is the hardest part.

Other goads to action include listing the advantages and disadvantages of getting the job done, setting specific deadlines, making a commitment to someone else, and promising yourself a reward.

My daughter Marilyn was cured of procrastination when she started dating a man who was even worse about it than she was. His lack of perspective—doing little, unnecessary things to evade important tasks—drove her crazy. It was an important lesson for her.

"I'm Late, I'm Late!"

Constant tardiness is another habit which adds to the pressure. When we are late for appointments, we are not only wasting our own time, but that of the person who's waiting for us. Being late for meetings causes late starts for everyone. We dash in, full of excuses, and waste more time getting ourselves together to begin.

We need to start early and allow plenty of time. The fact that a meeting is just fifteen minutes away when there's no traffic is meaningless if there's always traffic. Give yourself a ten-minute cushion. Take a book to read or work to do in your car if you arrive too soon. That way, you will waste neither your time nor that of anyone else.

Norvel used to pride himself on being the last person on the plane when we were leaving for a trip. Then, when ticket agents started giving away tickets ten minutes before the plane's scheduled departure, he learned to give himself extra time. Now we can relax and enjoy the trip.

The person who is constantly under pressure—feeling harried and hurried and rushing from one task to another—may seem the opposite of the procrastinator, but the results are much the same. Anxiety drains energy as well as wasting time. It wears us out without accomplishing anything.

If you're late, your mind is centered on getting there. If you aren't, you can think about other, more constructive things. A single-minded push is a waste of mental and emotional energies.

Telling ourselves that there isn't enough time can be a self-fulfilling prophecy. Have you ever tried pushing yourself on the computer, for instance? The faster you go and the tenser you get, the more mistakes you make and the longer it takes to do the job. Jesus never hurried, but he was always on time. God's Spirit slows us down. We need time to prepare, to think things through, to allow inspiration to grow, and to do the job well.

Surprisingly, slowing down doesn't necessarily mean we'll accomplish less. A few years ago, my doctor diagnosed a fluttery heart sensation I'd had since I was a child as tachycardia. He told me to cut out coffee, late hours, and stress. No stress? On a job with constant deadlines?

I was surprised to discover that I didn't have to get "charged up" to get things done. In fact, I had been wasting time in bluster. Of course, slowing down is not as easy as it sounds. You can slow to a walk and still be running inside. You can lie down to rest with your mind still racing.

You have to take it one step at a time. Find your own pace, and try not to crowd too much into a day.

Wasted Worry

Anxiety is often the result of feelings of inadequacy. It is symptomatic of prayerlessness and a lack of faith. It damages family life and undermines our Christian witness, disturbs our sleep, depresses our minds, and disfigures our faces.

Time spent in worry is time wasted. Two different surveys indicate that forty percent of the things we worry about never happen; we have no control over thirty-five percent of them; fifteen percent turn out better than we think they will, and eight percent are useless. Only two percent of the things we worry about are legitimate concerns!

Spiritual growth is one of the best ways of overcoming anxiety. When we really believe that our lives are in God's hands, that he cares about us and won't fail us, we can rest. "Trust in the Lord with all your heart and lean not on your own understanding" (Prov. 3:5). "Cast all your anxiety on him because he cares for you" (1 Peter 5:7).

Here are five steps to overcoming anxiety:

1. Pray

When you feel yourself worrying about something, turn it over to God in prayer. Pray and then forget it. It's God's problem now. "Do not be anxious about anything, but in everything, by prayer and petition, with thanksgiving, present your requests to God. And the peace of God, which transcends all understanding, will guard your hearts and your minds in Christ Jesus" (Phil. 4:6–7).

2. Work

Staying busy is another corrective for worry, but our activity should be planned, paced, and productive. Earl Riney wrote,

"Blessed is the man who is too busy to worry in the daytime and too sleepy at night."

3. Care

Become genuinely interested in other people. Their worries may put yours into better perspective, and thinking about them will get your mind off yourself.

4. Think

People who worry often do so because they have too many unfilled spaces in their minds. Fill those spaces with good things. Memorize Scripture and poetry. Enjoy the beauties of nature. Read uplifting biographies. "Whatever is true, whatever is noble, whatever is right, whatever is pure, whatever is lovely, whatever is admirable—if anything is excellent or praiseworthy—think about such things" (Phil. 4:8).

5. Wait

Often there is nothing we can do to make a situation better. Then we have to wait in faith. "They who wait for the Lord shall renew their strength, they shall mount up with wings like eagles, they shall run and not be weary, they shall walk and not faint" (Isa. 40:31 RSV).

Indecisiveness

A fourth way to kill time is to have trouble making up your mind. Have you ever had a pan on the stove and heard the baby crying in its crib? As you start toward the nursery, the doorbell rings. You turn toward it and the phone rings. You stand in the middle of the room, your mind spinning, not knowing which to do first.

If you're like most of us, you'll hesitate only a moment before moving. You run to the phone, ask the person to wait, then pick up the baby on the way to the door, hoping the food doesn't burn in the meantime. Or you might turn the stove off first, especially if it's your last pot of beans. Decisions are made

OVERCOMING WORRY
1. PRAY
2. WORK
3. CARE ABOUT OTHERS
4. THINK ABOUT GOOD THINGS
5. WAIT IN FAITH

on the basis of priorities—and how long we can keep something waiting without dire consequences.

Fear of making a wrong decision can keep us from making any decision at all. Accept the fact that you will make mistakes. It is better to decide to do something and do it—even if it's wrong—than to live your life in a state of indecision.

If you have time, it's good to think through a decision carefully, weighing the pros and cons. Collecting data and discussing the problem with others can be helpful. Of course, prayer characterized the periods before Jesus' major decisions— such as choosing his apostles and going to the cross—and it should characterize ours as well.

Set a deadline. Taking undue time to collect data and make a decision can be another means of procrastination or an indication of rigid perfectionism. Go ahead and take the first step, so you'll be committed to the course of action you've decided on. When you've made the decision in light of Bible knowledge, the counsel of Christian friends, prayer, and your own best reasoning, accept it as the will of God and put it into effect.

Decisions often have to be made without time for careful thought. Live in prayerful obedience, and trust your impulses.

Getting into the habit of doing certain jobs on particular days or at a particular time of day frees your mind from making unnecessary decisions. Outlining your plans and having options in mind will do the same. Charles W. Eliot of Harvard gave this advice: "When blocked or defeated in an enterprise I had much at heart, I always turned immediately to another field of work where progress looked possible, biding my time for a chance to resume the obstructed road."

By making more basic decisions, we establish priority systems for making many smaller ones. Conflict drains, particularly conflict of values. Elijah challenged the Israelites: "How long will you waver between two different opinions? If the Lord is God, follow him; but if Baal [or money or power or prestige] is God, follow him" (1 Kings 18:21).

Feeding Anger

Anger is another time- and energy-waster. Repressed anger can make us chronically tired. Solomon first noted the connection between anger and energy. "He that is slow to anger is better than the mighty," he said, "and he that ruleth his spirit than he that taketh a city" (Prov. 16:32 KJV).

At one time, psychologists felt that expression was the best solution to the problem of anger, but now they are revising their assessment. Carol Tavris, author of *Anger: The Misunderstood Emotion*, has found that telling someone off, for instance, does not reduce anger. Basically, suppressing anger can allow stress to continue, but expressing it can create even more stress. We can anger others and start a fight. Even if we discuss our anger with someone who agrees with us, it can feed on itself and grow instead of disappearing.

One way to deal with anger is to avoid anger-producing situations. Another is to work it off in harmless activities. It's better to hit a tennis ball than the boss's head! Relaxing and thinking good thoughts can do wonders. Calmly expressing your anger can be better than nursing a grudge.

The most important lesson we can learn is the difference

between trivial angers, which are best forgotten, and important ones, which need to be discussed and dealt with.

Entertaining Ourselves to Death

A CBS survey of time use indicates that, out of 168 hours a week, the average person spends 8 1/2 hours eating, 26 1/2 hours working, 58 hours sleeping, and 57 hours in leisure activities. Watching TV and listening to the radio, tapes, or CDs account for 49 hours of the average person's leisure activity time. Since most of us work considerably more than 26 1/2 hours a week, some of us must be living in front of the TV!

Mark Crispin, in an article in *Harper's*, wrote that TV is on over seven hours a day in the average household—influencing our buying habits and stimulating our desires even when we aren't aware of it. "TV begins by offering us a beautiful hallucination of diversity," Crispin says. "But it is finally like a drug whose high is only the conviction that its user is too cool to be addicted."

Television is habit-forming, but habits can be broken. Some have gone so far as to take the TV out of the house. That is one solution, but it may not be the best. There are many informative and entertaining programs on television. The key is selectivity. We should check the offerings, choose one or two good programs, and limit our viewing to those.

We can use our imaginations to come up with alternate activities. How about reading, family fun and discussions, crafts or hobbies, good deeds, exercise, prayer?

An occasional vacation is rejuvenating, but constant week-ending can waste time and wear you out. With so many recreational opportunities available, we must be wise and balanced in our choices.

Are You Killing Time?

To determine if you are making the best use of your time, keep a time log—a detailed list of how you spend your hours in any given week. List the days of the week across the top of the page, and the time of day by half-hour increments down the left-hand margin.

Breaking Habits

Psychologists suggest that it takes three weeks to establish a habit and three weeks to break one. To break one of my bad habits, I will

1. pinpoint the habit which is hindering me and write it down together with my resolve to eliminate it.

2. visualize my work with this habit eliminated in order to motivate my new behavior.

3. ask someone close to me for support in forming a new habit.

4. allow no exception to my new resolve.

5. when I fail, put it behind me and renew my resolve.

6. endure the pain of changing my work habits in order to grow.

Record what you actually did in a given time period. Do not wait until evening to enter your activities. You want the facts, not blurred memories.

This is not an easy exercise. Don't succumb to the temptation to write it off as an unusual week, or to crowd in a quiet time just so you can enter it in the log. Be scrupulously honest. No deception.

Keep your own record so you know it's right. You may be disappointed to realize how little time you spend with your family or with the Lord. Or how much time you are spending on TV or shopping or on the phone. Perhaps you thought that other people were planning your time and found that, in reality, it was your own lack of decision. Most of us discover that the process of living takes up most of our time (in spite of labor-saving devices). Perhaps you have less discretionary time than you thought.

Now you can consider changes. When you know where you are and where you want to be, you can make plans to progress toward your destination.

Killing time is a violent pursuit. As Christians we are committed to respect life and the time life is made of, and to use it wisely. We can reduce drudgery and increase productivity by

How I Spend My Time

	7	8	9	10	11	12	1	2	3	4	5	6	7	8	9	10
Worship																
Sleep																
Meals																
Travel																
Job																
Home																
Family																
Recreation																
Grooming																

Check one square every half hour. (You may have 2 checks per square.)

rooting out counterproductive habits and attitudes and developing tolerance, decisiveness, and self-discipline. Life becomes an adventure when we learn to trust God, ourselves, and one another.

But growth is painful. A lobster has to shed its shell to grow and is vulnerable until a new shell forms. We have to shed old, unworkable habits and risk letting people discover that we don't always do everything right. But we'll gain in the long run by having a fuller, more satisfying life.

As Stephen Vincent Benet wrote:

> Life is not lost by dying! Life is lost
> Minute by minute, day by dragging day
> In all the thousand small, uncaring ways.

Questions and Activities

1. Think back over the ways of killing time listed in this chapter. Which problem most plagues you? Reread that section and incorporate one suggestion for overcoming it.

2. What jobs do you need to do today that demand your best efforts? Which can get by with less?

3. What disagreeable task have you been postponing? Determine to spend just five minutes on it today.

4. Allow yourself a ten-minute cushion before every appointment this week and see if it doesn't reduce stress.

5. Keep a log of the way you spend your time for the next three weeks. Are you wasting time or using it effectively?

6
My Work

"Go to the ant ..."
—Proverbs 6:6

Getting ready for Christmas is always exciting and exhausting. Beginning on December 1, we order our twelve-foot tree and get out all the boxes of tree ornaments, candles, indoor and outdoor lights, and all the other decorations we've collected since we married. Our wonderful neighbor, Jamie, who is an interior decorator, makes our house look special. Then we begin baking decorated cookies, date nut bread, and carrot cake, and making fudge and candied walnuts. We slice fruitcakes, make vegetable trees and salmon molds, and arrange plates of cheeses and fruit trays. Finally, we're ready for our annual open house, which is usually the second Sunday in December.

When all the preparations are made, I can relax and enjoy my family and friends. After all, that's the point of my efforts. It would be terrible if the end result of all our work were just to keep a house clean or to make money. The result of most work is to bring joy into the lives of those we love.

Yet job dissatisfaction is one of the most pervasive problems in American business. Polls indicate that as many as forty percent of all workers are dissatisfied. Management consultant Roy Walters maintains that "very few people . . . are truly excited about their daily work. . . . They're bored 'out of their tree'; they're going crazy."

According to psychiatrist Robert Coles, "Working people . . . feel cornered, trapped, lonely, pushed around at work and confused by a sense of meaninglessness." Their lack of

enthusiasm results in absenteeism, tardiness, limited produc-
tion, and alcohol and drug abuse.

Work is not just a job that brings in a salary. It is anything we
put effort into. Whether your task is business, homemaking,
schoolwork, service or ministry—or more likely some combination of the above—why do you do the work you do? Because you
need the money? Because you're afraid of what people will say if
you don't work? Because you want to stay busy? Because you
want to be a "good Christian"? Or because you love God and
other people?

When God created the first people, before sin entered the
world, he gave them dominion over the rest of his creation
(Gen. 1:26-28), and he gave them work to do (2:15). The earth
and all its wealth belongs to God. We are his stewards. We have
a part in the ongoing task of rebuilding the earth. We share
God's work of bringing order out of chaos—whether setting up a
filing system, cleaning out the garage, or teaching a child.

God expects us to work. "Six days you shall labor and do all
your work" (Ex. 20:9). God's commands are always for our good.
As Charles Kingsley wrote, "Thank God every morning when
you get up that you have something to do which must be done,
whether you like it or not. Being forced to work, and forced to
do your best, will breed in you temperance, self-control,
diligence, strength of will, and a hundred other virtues which
the idle never know."

As a matter of fact, most people consider work essential to
happiness. Surveys indicate that people who are happy with
their work are happier people. Working makes you feel good
about yourself.

Work can also be a form of worship. Hands cannot forever be
folded in prayer. Someone must get Sally to the dentist and
Bobby to school. Husbands require clean shirts. There are
luncheon appointments and letters to write, guests to receive,
phones to answer, contracts to sign and dishes to do, meetings to
attend, clothes to mend, sales to make, lessons to study, flowers
to plant. We should make our tasks a part of devotional living.
Our Father is not uninterested in any of them. He is the Lord of
every moment.

How do we make our work a part of our service to God? "Go

to the ant, you sluggard; consider its ways and be wise!" (Prov. 6:6).

Let God Set the Task

Like birds, which fly great distances over regular routes without a compass, or beavers, who build engineering marvels without a plan, ants operate by instinct. They are perfectly attuned to God's will for them. We, too, should work according to God's dictates. For only when we work as God intends do we find fulfillment as human beings, and only then is our work truly effective.

Richard Foster, author of *Celebration of Discipline* and *Freedom of Simplicity*, explains that "discipline . . . is being responsive to God in my life." Without that discipline, we easily fall prey to one of two extremes: rigidity (being so structured that we can only see one way of doing things) or anarchy (being totally unstructured).

"One of the acts of discipline," according to Foster, "is saying no. . . . Most of us could cut twenty percent of what we do without reducing our output one iota." Explaining how he and his wife decided how many speaking engagements he could accept without neglecting his responsibilities as a husband and father, Foster assures us that, if we delete everything from our schedules that is not God's will for us, we will be left with a manageable task. "Not everything we tackle is something God wants accomplished," he says.

My Work

Home
cooking
cleaning
laundry
shopping
errands

Family
teaching
enjoying
disciplining
encouraging

Career
planning
assigning
writing
editing
corresponding

Church
teaching
giving seminars
serving

Personal
grooming
entertaining
corresponding
studying

We belong to God. "For we are God's workmanship, created in Christ Jesus to do good works" (Eph. 2:10). Our holy assignment is not just to get God to help us, but to turn our wills over to him and ask him to let us assist him with his purposes.

When we depend on our own efforts rather than God's grace to set our work load, we may be working for money or status, to justify our existence or gain acceptance, to impress God or others. None of these motivations is worthy of the child of God.

Take the Broad View

Ants are social insects, living together in highly organized communities. Each ant has specialized duties to perform for the benefit of the community as a whole.

Part of the problem of work in today's world is that we fail to see the relationship between our specific job and the broader society. As Paul Tournier points out in his book, *The Adventure of Living,*

Most people live their whole lives within the limits of a narrow specialization, hardly ever even glimpsing its relationships with other spheres of life. . . . They know their jobs well and work at them carefully and conscientiously. They may even excel at them, and, because of the very perfection of their technical skill, never feel in the slightest degree that what they are engaged in is still an adventure.

We need to take a broader view—to see that the calculator we produce will help some woman keep account of her monthly bills; the child we rear will become a contributing part of society; the report we type will help our organization better serve its customers; the house we sell will be home to a family.

The end is always people. This was true in the life of Jesus. He made water into wine at the wedding feast, not just to show his power, but to relieve his host's anxiety, to please his mother, and to enhance the enjoyment of the guests.

Most of us have committed ourselves not to engage in any occupation or endeavor that brings harm to others. But we need to go a step beyond that and commit ourselves only to those tasks which contribute something worthwhile to the general welfare. If we can see no possible benefit to anybody from the work we are doing, we should look for something else.

If you take the broad view, you may be surprised to discover how important your work is. Dr. Rene Dubois, author and microbiologist, sees the broader implications of her work: "Just the excitement of seeking something new is a satisfaction that hardly any other occupation gives. . . . I have learned to relate my scientific preoccupation to the larger problems of the world."

So does the bus driver on a commuter route who says, "This city runs because I bring the guys who make the decisions in each morning and home every night." Both have learned something from the ant. What else can we learn from this industrious creature?

Take the Initiative

Solomon says that the ant works with "no commander, no overseer or ruler" (Prov. 6:7). Ants perform their tasks independently. They're self-starters. Nobody has to stand over them, telling them what to do.

How many of us are that self-motivated? How many of us work as hard when the boss is not around as we do when she is? Paul tells us that our real boss is always there. We aren't working for people alone, but for the Lord (Col. 3:22–24).

According to Tournier, our problems result from the fact that "we all make this harmful distinction between our professional lives and our spiritual lives. To unite them once more is to restore to both the quality of an adventure, or rather to make of them one great adventure instead of two: the adventure of the incarnation of the Spirit in concrete reality."

In his own experience as a doctor, Tournier found that he had divided the two parts of his life. He would spend his usual time in consultation with a patient, then ask him to return in the evening for a talk.

> I was thus living two quite distinct lives, the classical practice of scientific medicine in the daytime and a fireside medicine in the evening—a situation which clearly enough expressed the division . . . between the domain of science and that of morality.
>
> Well, I felt myself called to unite these two lives, to follow my adventure of faith within my work and not outside it. For it was soon apparent that when a fireside chat helped a patient to solve his personal problems it also contributed as much as medicine, dieting, or the lancet to the healing of his condition.

Another danger is to make distinctions between types of work. John Gardner, former Secretary of Health, Education and Welfare, says, "The society which scorns excellence in plumbing because plumbing is a humble activity and tolerates shoddiness in philosophy because it is an exalted activity will have neither good plumbing nor good philosophy. Neither its pipes nor its theories will hold water."

No job is too humble to be elevated by a good attitude. A tombstone in an English churchyard reads, "Here lies the body of Thomas Cobb, who made shoes to the glory of God for fifty years."

Much of our work is routine. At least three-fourths of the time spent by the president of a large corporation is spent doing things an unskilled laborer can do. Don't regret routine, accept it. If you hate the boredom of doing the same task over and over, tension mounts. Tension is relieved when you gladly accept your task.

Someone asked a man, "Do you like to drive?" He thought a minute and said, "I neither like it nor dislike it—I drive."

Work need not be drudgery, something to discharge before getting on to something more interesting. We may be suffering from a dearth of creativity, but much of our work—whether making a dress, decorating a room, writing a book, or preparing a lesson—can sizzle with excitement if we bring heart and a little imagination to the task.

God himself is a worker. He spent six days creating the world and then rested on the seventh. "My Father is working still," Jesus said, "and I am working" (John 5:17 RSV). Our work can be a communion with him.

Look Ahead

The ant is a prudent creature. "It stores its provisions in summer and gathers its food at harvest" (Prov. 6:8). The well-known tale of "The Grasshopper and the Ant" illustrates the value of foresight, as the ant gathers food for the winter while the grasshopper plays. When the cold winds blow, the grasshopper is starving, but the ant has enough for itself and to spare.

There are several ways we can benefit from foresight. We can look ahead and plan our work itself, dividing the tasks into a series of distinct beginnings and ends. We can incorporate as much latitude for self-expression and personal decision as possible. We can build evaluation into the job. Are we improving in ability? speed? efficiency?

Read and think with an eye to the future. Store observations, make notes, keep files of ideas for future use.

We save time by thinking ahead. I remember the first time I stayed in the dormitory during the Bible Lectureship at Pepperdine. I roomed with a friend, and we shared a bathroom with a suite of several other rooms. The first morning, when I went down to brush my teeth, I found I had left my washcloth and soap, so I had to go back before I could shower. Then I realized I'd forgotten my towel, and then my shampoo. I was so late I had

to bolt my breakfast and slip in after the first class had started. The next morning, I thought through the steps it would take to get ready and had all my items together in a bag when I went down to the bathroom. I saved enough time getting ready that I was able to enjoy a leisurely breakfast and still get to class with time to spare.

One of our teachers in high school used to tell us, "Use your head and save your feet." I apply the principle to straightening the house. When I'm in one room, I gather as many items as I can to take to the next.

This principle can be applied to many areas. Ernest Hemingway generally wrote five hundred words a day. However, when he was working on *The Old Man and the Sea*, he was surprised to discover that he was writing a thousand words a day. His increased speed was the result of planning ahead. He had been writing the book in his mind for sixteen years!

Finally, plan your overall work life. Consider where you want to go and what steps you can take to get there. Don't just drift. Early retirement presents the challenge of a second career if you prepare by beginning it as a hobby before retirement comes. Women who work solely at home need to realize that they can count on some thirty productive years after the children are grown. Begin early to develop the skills and interests which will make that time worthwhile.

My Career History and Projection

Past
1. Helped my father on weekly newspaper.
2. Edited student newspaper.
3. Did publicity for Christian colleges.
4. Became editorial assistant for *20th Century Christian.*
5. Became associate editor of *20th Century Christian.*
6. Began *God Has . . .* series.
7. Wrote novel.
8. Wrote time management book.

(I am basically satisfied with my career, but here you may want to veer off into an entirely new area. Let your dreams be your guide.)

Future
1. Market novel.
2. Add to *God Has . . .* series.
3. Write other books of fiction and nonfiction.
4. Read and perfect skills.
5. Travel and learn more background material (architecture, botany).
6. Work with other writers.

Be Industrious

Aleksandr Solzhenitsyn, in *The Gulag Archipelago,* explains what he calls "stretching the rubber." A prisoner in a labor camp in the Soviet Union would never openly refuse an order. He'd listen carefully, nod his head, and start off to do the task. However, he would never complete it. Sometimes he wouldn't even begin.

"All they were on the lookout for was ways to spoil their footgear—and not go out to work; how to wreck a crane, to buckle a wheel, to break a spade, to sink a pail—anything for a pretext to sit down and smoke."

Understandably, these prisoners were poorly motivated. But

how many of us "stretch the rubber" when we accept a job and then don't do our best?

Ants have been known to carry loads several times their size. Observing their industry, Solomon exclaimed, "How long will you lie there, you sluggard? When will you get up from your sleep?" (Prov. 6:9).

God calls industrious people. When God called, Moses was watching his flock, Elijah was plowing, Gideon was threshing wheat, David was caring for sheep, Peter and Andrew were fishing, James and John were mending nets, Matthew was collecting taxes, and the Samaritan woman was drawing water from a well.

That is not to say that God calls workaholics. Workaholics are compulsive people who are pressured by time and feel guilty when they aren't working. They let work drain energy that could be devoted to enjoyment and service.

God calls us to work, but he doesn't call us to all the jobs which might be done. When we are frantically busy, we probably are not trusting him and listening for his instructions. Frenzy isn't efficient. Busyness actually reduces the quality of our work.

As public relations executive Richard R. Conarroe put it, "Many busy people could get their jobs done more easily, better, and often in a lot less time if they would stop working so hard."

One salesman, who noted that he made most of his sales before noon, worked out a schedule whereby he made all his sales calls in the morning and spent the afternoon with his sons. His sales increased.

Richard Foster says that "the disciplined person is the person who does what needs to be done when it needs to be done . . . who lives life appropriately." Workaholism shows a lack of discipline and can, according to Foster, result from a "desperate need for approval."

Time without energy is useless. Budget your energy. Do demanding jobs when you're fresh. Pace yourself. A mile runner doesn't burn herself out in the first quarter. We can't go full speed without depleting our physical, mental, emotional, and spiritual energy. Change pace. When you get tired of thinking, do something physical. Divide tasks into easy-to-finish segments. A sense of progress helps increase energy. Drill for skill. The greater your skill, the less fatiguing a job will be. When you've done something a particular way thirty-five times, it becomes a habit. Once routine tasks become habitual, you can do them with less thought and effort.

Efficiency falters for all of us after about forty-eight hours a week (an average six-day workweek). When possible, stop short of fatigue, though it takes a wise woman to know the difference between fatigue and laziness. We all run the risk of becoming lazy. Pampered and well-fed, lulled by television, with increasing salaries for a decreasing workweek, many of us don't know what to do with our leisure time. We need the challenge of the industrious ant.

Damon Stetson, in a *New York Times* article, cited a survey showing that a cross-section of office employees were producing only fifty-five percent of their potential. Reasons included slow starts in the morning, extended coffee breaks, socializing, long lunches, and getting ready to leave before the end of the workday.

We need to get tough with ourselves and discipline ourselves to work hard. "Whatever your hand finds to do, do it with all your might" (Eccl. 9:10). Brisk movements save time and lift the spirits. Ride your personal cycles of energy, enthusiasm, and creativity. Use lower energy periods to plan and store up energy for future use.

Paul warns young widows against wasting their time "being idle and going about from house to house," becoming "gossips and busybodies, saying things they ought not to" (1 Tim. 5:13). The worthy woman is commended for her diligence; she "does not eat the bread of idleness" (Prov. 31:27).

A lazy employee is in danger of losing her job, the idle farmer will not produce a crop, the busybody homemaker will find things falling apart at home. "A little sleep, a little slumber, a little folding of the hands to rest—and poverty will come on you like a bandit and scarcity like an armed man" (Prov. 6:10–11).

The lazy person has trouble feeling good about herself and is of little good to others. In fact, she may be tempted to live off the productivity of others. Paul has a solution for this problem: "He who has been stealing must steal no longer, but must work, doing something useful with his own hands, that he may have something to share with those in need" (Eph. 4:28). This isn't just the Protestant work ethic. It's the ethic of Christ, who "went around doing good" (Acts 10:38).

Take Pride in Your Work

Our ability to benefit from our work, to work joyfully and experience true fulfillment, depends to a great extent on our attitude toward our work. A poll taken by *USA Today* indicates that people feel better about their work when they consider it a career rather than just a job.

This fact is an argument against urging women to concentrate on their families by considering their jobs as necessary evils. It's devastating to anyone to denigrate a task they spend a sizable part of their week doing.

It is also an argument against tearing down those who choose and are able to work full time in their homes. All of us need to feel good about the work we do.

Whatever your occupation, take pride in a job well done. Work creatively. Look for ways to enrich the experience. Establish good relations with employers, employees, and co-workers. And study for the next step. You will find more satisfaction and a closer tie between your secular and spiritual selves.

God tells us we should do whatever we do with our might and for his glory. As Dorothy L. Sayers put it, in our work our nature "should find its proper exercise and delight and so fulfill itself to the glory of God."

And Henry Van Dyke encourages us to accept whatever work is ours to do:

> Let me but do my work from day to day,
> In field or forest, at the desk or loom,
> In roaring market-place or tranquil room;
> Let me but find it in my heart to say,
> When vagrant wishes beckon me astray,

"This is my work; my blessing, not my doom;
Of all who live, I am the one by whom
This work can best be done in the right way."

Then shall I see it not too great, nor small,
To suit my spirit and to prove my powers,
Then shall I turn, when the long shadows fall
At eventide, to play and love and rest,
Because I know for me my work is best.

Questions and Activities

1. What different tasks go together to make up the work you do each day?

2. Are you satisfied with your work? Why or why not?

3. How does your work serve people—both immediately and in a broader sense?

4. Trace your career history. Now project the line. What can you look forward to in the future? What kinds of work would you enjoy doing? How can you start preparing now?

5. Do you do your work to the glory of God? How can you do so more consciously?

7
My Scraps of Time

> *"Who despises the day of
> small things?"*
> *—Zechariah 4:10*

My granny used to make piecework quilts—brightly colored coverlets with intricate designs—from scraps of cloth left over from sewing. I still have one, though it's frayed around the edges, that is over thirty years old. How warm and cozy it feels on winter mornings, and what fun to lie under it and study the prints and pattern. It's called "Bird at the Window," and I can still see the scrap from an old skirt of mine, a blouse of my mother's, and a dress my sister wore when she was just a child.

Granny also made piecework aprons and rag rugs and pictures out of shells. In fact, I think she could find a use for almost anything! She saw the potential in things that most people would throw away, and she had the patience and imagination to make something of worth and beauty from them.

Odd bits of time are another potentially valuable commodity which many waste. As Caleb C. Colton pointed out, "Much may be done in those little shreds and patches of time, which every day produces, and which most men [and women] throw away, but which nevertheless will make at the end of it no small deduction from the life."

A study conducted by the University of Wisconsin indicates that the average person spends three years of his life waiting. A Gallup poll of one hundred randomly selected individuals showed that they all expected to spend some time waiting during the next few hours, but only one in eight had planned anything constructive to do during that time.

Scraps of time have great potential, but many of us ignore them. When a group of people were asked what they did when waiting for an overdue visitor or a meeting or for someone to call back, their answers ranged from "I don't know—never thought about it" to "I doodle" or "I twist paper clips." "Most people do not think in terms of minutes," time expert Alan Lakein tells us. "They waste all their minutes."

The Value of Five Minutes

People who have made an impact on the world have always recognized the worth of even small scraps of time. "The reason I beat the Austrians," Napoleon said, "is that they did not know the value of five minutes."

"Fill-In" Jobs

In five minutes I can:
  water a plant
  gaze out the window
  read a poem
  list people to call or write
  give someone a hug
  thank God for something

In ten minutes I can:
  write a note or post card
  look over my calendar
  count my blessings
  list errands to run
  read a story to a child
  pray God's blessings on a special concern

In fifteen minutes I can:
  call a sick friend
  read a chapter or two in the Bible
  walk around the block
  write a letter
  organize a drawer
  read a chapter in a good book
  start a long-range project

When he had a job selling sandwiches on a passenger train, Thomas Edison set up a lab in the baggage car and worked on experiments between his trips down the aisles.

Robert Louis Stevenson always carried two books—one to

read and one to take notes in—so he could make good use of spare minutes.

William Lyon Phelps wrote letters to people during odd bits of time between appointments.

A professional writer once made a survey of what he could do with the scraps of five minutes or less that a week's time produced—that is, five minutes waiting for his wife, five minutes waiting for a bus, five minutes between appointments, etc. He found he could dream, write a few notes in his writer's notebook, read a few pages in a book, look up a word in a dictionary and follow its related meanings, craft a sentence or paragraph or a bit of dialogue.

Businesspeople can use the time between meetings, or even the time they're waiting on hold on the telephone, to sort through their "in" boxes, organize filing chores, plan calls, read trade magazines and memos, update forms or calendars, think, plan and recharge.

Jim Bill dictates letters on a tape recorder when he's in the car. Ala Beth makes drapes while talking on the phone. Helen made 11,500 dolls to sell to benefit Christian education, mostly in her spare time.

Someone has written,

> Could you spare five minutes of one day to embrace its honest meaning?
> Could you spare five minutes to give a soft answer, turn the other cheek, do unto others as you would be done by?
> Could you spare five minutes to protect the weak, defend the persecuted, comfort those who mourn, and love your neighbor as yourself?
> Could you spare five minutes to feed the hungry, invite the stranger, cherish a child?
> Could you spare five minutes to tender mercy, give without hope of receiving, and forgive those who know not what they do?
> Could you spare five minutes to cast out fear, choose between good and evil, and let your light shine?
> Could you spare five minutes from one thousand four hundred and forty to reach at least slightly beyond the confining boundaries of self, to emerge from concerns determined by greed and prejudice, to depart the cheerless

abode of cynicism and disdain, to cease the aimless drifting toward paths of ease?

Could you spare five minutes to care?

In five minutes, you can count your blessings, hug your husband, look out the window as far as possible and then close your eyes and dream, quote Scriptures to yourself, enjoy a child's laughter, a neighbor's friendly greeting, or the beauty of the day.

In ten minutes, you can call and invite a friend to worship, write a note to a sick friend, or read a story to a child.

In only fifteen minutes a day, you can read the entire Bible through in one year.

But you can't do much with scraps of time if you don't prepare for them in advance. Make a list of tasks you can do in brief time periods. Henry Haddow advises that we pack our time as we would pack a suitcase, "filling up the small places with small things."

My list includes exercising, reading, mending, planning a new writing project, praying, cleaning out a drawer, writing a letter, trimming my nails, looking over my calendar, cleaning out a file, and counting my blessings.

The point of using your scraps of time is not to be furiously active every moment of the day. There is also the beauty of the five-minute rest. To lie down and put your feet up for even five minutes can provide a welcome lift in the middle of a grueling schedule. When you're physically tired, it can be restful to make calls, do planning, or read. When you're mentally exhausted, try cleaning windows, or doing carpentry work, or finishing a small garden task. A change is often as good as a rest.

We are wasting something precious when we waste time, and we are erring even more if we spend it fretting. When someone is running late for an appointment, embrace that extra time as God's special gift to you. When you are stuck in traffic, enjoy the flowers by the roadside.

On our way to Malibu recently, traffic came to a halt just outside the Santa Monica tunnel. For the next forty minutes, we just sat there, inching forward only a mile or two. We expected to see tempers flare, but as we watched the people around us, we saw several get out of their cars and visit with each other. One woman walked her baby up and down the roadside. Drivers pulled back to make room for help to get to a motorist whose car had overheated.

My husband and I had a good talk for the first time in a busy week. Then we turned on the radio to see what had happened. When we heard about the accident ahead, I prayed for those who were hurt and for the friends and family of those who had died.

We were late getting to Malibu, but we were grateful that we'd made it at all—something we seldom stop to think about. We thought of our kind and friendly "fellow-waiters" with appreciation. And we sorrowed for those who were hurting. It was a tragic and unexpected delay, but there were blessings in it.

Minutes Add Up

As mighty rocks are eroded by small drops of water, massive tasks can be accomplished, little by little, in scraps of time. According to Peter Marshall, "Most of the world's great men [and women] have achieved their true life work, not in the course of their needful occupations, but in their spare time."

After David Livingstone worked from 6 A.M. until 8 P.M. in a Dumbarton cotton mill, he spent his evenings studying Latin. He was able to read Horace and Virgil by the time he was sixteen, and by age twenty-seven, he had taken courses in medicine and theology.

And how many women have produced outstanding works of art during their babies' naps and between running errands for older children?

John Erskine, well-known author, professor, and lecturer, learned the lesson of using scraps of time at age fourteen when his piano teacher asked him how long he practiced at any one sitting.

"An hour or more," he said.

"Don't do that," she said. "When you grow up, time won't come in long stretches. Practice in minutes, whenever you can find them—five or ten before school, after lunch, between chores. Spread the practice throughout the day, and music will become a part of your life."

When he was older, Erskine applied her advice to other areas. He wrote most of his book, *Helen of Troy*, on streetcars commuting to the university where he taught.

When A. Michael Ramsey, the Archbishop of Canterbury, was asked when he found time to write, he replied: "Monday, a quarter of an hour; Tuesday, ten minutes; Wednesday, rather better, half an hour; Thursday not very good, but ten minutes; Friday a bit of a lull, an hour; Saturday, half an hour."

Most jobs can be broken into bite-sized portions. But it takes organization to be able to pick up work where we left it. My mother-in-law keeps handwork and sewing supplies in a basket near at hand for easy access when she has spare time. I keep a notebook or folder for each project I'm working on and all my materials in handy reach. Then, when I have a block of time— small or large—I can get right to work.

Spiritual growth, as well, comes gradually, a bit at a time. If we wait until we have a spare hour to study the Bible, pray, or do a kind deed, we may never get around to it. But if we take the moments that come, day by day, spiritual thoughts and activities will permeate our lives and shine out to enrich the lives of others.

That's the way the Israelites were to teach God's laws to their children: "Talk about them when you sit at home and when you walk along the road, when you lie down and when you get up" (Deut. 6:7).

The secret is persistence—taking the opportunities that present themselves and doing a little at a time. Great things are accomplished in small acts. "Who despises the day of small things?" (Zech. 4:10). It's our attitude toward small opportunities, and the great number of them which make up each of our days, that makes the difference.

Specific Suggestions

Where do we find these scraps of time? When we're on hold on the phone, waiting at a stoplight, in the doctor's office, commuting. When we have a few minutes before we need to leave the house, when we're waiting for our husbands to come to bed, when we can't sleep.

Someone has estimated that most of us will spend over a year of our lives just waiting in lines—at the post office, the bank, the Department of Motor Vehicles, the Social Security office, the passport office. Lines are a fact of life.

When we're sitting, it's easy to make good use of waiting time. It's harder when we're standing up, but Patrick Connolly of the Nashville *Tennessean* suggests using that time to read an article clipped from a magazine, jot a note on a stamped post card, or do isometric exercises. We can also plan our schedule, balance our checkbook, pray, and study the people around us.

Elsie prays at stoplights. When the light changes, she pulls away refreshed, not harried as she would be if she'd sat there drumming her fingers. Betty listens to tapes of the Bible, hymns, and lectures during her forty-minute commute to and from work each day. In this way, she decides where her mind will be rather than allowing the radio to dictate. We can sing hymns, praise God for his goodness, ask him for his forgiveness, and contemplate his love. Time alone in our cars is a good time to practice mind renewal (Rom. 12:2).

Marla bought a small, voice-activated tape recorder to dictate notes to herself while she's driving. I try to take a book I'm reading to the doctor's office. I'd rather be doing my own work than glancing through old magazines. But if I'm stuck with the magazines, I copy recipes and housekeeping tips from them.

Other suggestions include the following:

1. Keep note pads and paper in various rooms, in purse or pocket, and in your car. You can jot reminders to yourself, plan Bible class lessons, or start grocery lists.
2. Get to work quickly. It's easy to waste time deciding what, if anything, to do with it.
3. Be sure to keep plenty of reading material at hand, and develop the habit of picking up a book when you go out the door.
4. Learn to do two things at once. Pray, plan, dictate, or listen to tapes while driving. The Ethiopian eunuch made good use of his travel time (Acts 8:28). Mend, do handwork, exercise, or catch up scrapbooks and photo albums while watching TV.
5. Keep stationery, post cards, or note cards and a pen in your purse. One woman was delighted to discover that,

almost overnight, she was writing letters and notes of appreciation to friends and acquaintances—even congressmen!

6. Pack your own "spare time" bag. It can include mending or a needlework project, a book you've been intending to read, letters that need to be answered, pen and paper, your address book (and scraps of paper you've jotted addresses on which need to be copied into it), recipes to file—anything that will fit well into scraps of time. Keep it handy. Take it with you. Use it. You may be surprised what you can accomplish.

Contents of a "Spare Time" Bag

1. mending or needlework project
2. book, notebook, and pen
3. letters, pen and paper, address book, stamps
4. recipes clipped from magazines and newspapers, note cards, pen
5. files to cull
6. scrapbook and box of photos or mementos

God's Interruptions

No matter how tightly you pack your time, be prepared for God's interruptions. Some non-priority items will have to be eliminated to allow for them, but these interruptions may be your greatest opportunities for service. They may be God's way of tapping you on the shoulder.

One day I had a number of tasks to do that I felt were important until I heard that a sister in the church had lost her home and everything in it by fire. Suddenly my plans seemed small and insignificant.

Often, during the course of a mother's day, she is tempted to say to her child, "Run on now. I don't have time." No matter how tempted you are, think the next time before you say these words to your child. Life with our children is so short—just a couple of precious decades. That mother is wise who, in the middle of important work, stops to hug her daughter or to look her son in the eye and hear him out. No moment in the life of a child is unimportant, and one primary task of mothers is to communicate to children that they are loved.

Wise, as well, is the woman who takes time to listen to the concerns of her husband or friend. Norvel sometimes asks, "Are you listening?" when it is obvious that I'm trying to do something else at the same time. One of the greatest compliments I can pay him is to be totally present in a situation. I can put down my paper or book and concentrate on what he's saying, resisting the temptation to let my mind wander or to plan what I'm going to say in reply.

The wise woman knows what is important. If you don't get the dress finished because you baked cookies with your child, if you have to stay a little late at work because a coworker needs to talk, if a few things are left undone because you take a dish to a sick friend or watch a sunset with your husband, what harm is there?

The telephone is one of the most intrusive machines ever invented. It has no regard for the importance of our work. It rings just as insistently when someone wants to gossip or to sell something as it does in an emergency. Many people have installed answering machines—not merely to get messages when they are away, but also to screen messages while they are at home.

While answering devices are convenient and may even be necessary in some cases, we Christians ought to consider seriously our need to be available to others. The priest and the Levite were on a tight schedule (Luke 10:30–35); they had things that needed to be done. Only the Good Samaritan was willing to be interrupted, to lay aside his plans when he met Jesus in that battered form on the roadside.

Machines, too, do not always operate efficiently. Into every life comes the stopped-up sink, the "down" computer, and the dead battery. Emergencies are a part of all our lives. To resent them is to build up frustration.

And what about illness, accident, or injury? When we find ourselves flat on our backs, do we know how to use this time, as my friend Willa does, to grow closer to God? Or do we become impatient and blame him for interrupting our plans? Do we use it to minister to others with phone calls or cards, or do we lie there feeling sorry for ourselves? Do we take the opportunity to learn patience and develop character, or do we snap at our families and expect to be waited on?

All emergencies require a change in timing. They take minutes away from something else we had planned to do. They crowd our hours, cause us to rearrange our schedules, and demand flexibility. We need elasticity. If we are brittle or unbending, we will break. We need the sort of flexibility a rubber ball has which enables it to give with the pressure and bounce back. We need to be able to cope with an emergency and then recover quickly when the trying time is over.

An emergency is a divine interruption designed to test our character and see whether we can control ourselves with forbearance and love. God will help us gain the flexibility we need to deal constructively with the interruptions he gives us.

Make friends of interruptions. There is an opportunity in each one—to respond with love or with impatience, to learn flexibility or become more unbending, to do God's work or our own, to examine our priorities or feel put upon.

Jesus was on his way to heal Jairus's daughter when a woman with a hemorrhage touched the hem of his garment (Matt. 9:18–25). He could have thought, "I'm on my way to save a life. I'm in a hurry." But he said yes when he might have said no. Jesus took the time—to pick up a child, to heal a long-forgotten lame man, to feed a multitude.

Only God can tell where we are needed. Our lives, our feet, our thoughts, our resources are his equipment. Our minutes are important, for they are God's minutes—to use as we have planned or as he sees fit. When we become aware of the value of our scraps of time and start finding productive and satisfying ways to fill them, we may find that we are able to manage all our time better. The urgency of doing so is pointed out in this poem by an unknown author:

> I have only just a minute,
>   Just sixty seconds in it,
> Forced upon me, can't refuse it,
>   Didn't seek it, didn't choose it,

Must suffer if I lose it,
   Give account if I abuse it,
Just a tiny minute,
   But eternity is in it.

Questions and Activities

1. Where do you do most of your waiting? How could you better prepare for it?

2. List tasks you could do in five, ten, or fifteen spare minutes. How could you organize your materials to maximize time?

3. What long-range projects have you been putting off because you didn't have time? Could you do one in brief increments?

4. What can you do as a passenger in a car? as the driver?

5. What interruptions have you experienced, and what did God teach you from them?

8
Time Out

> *"Be still, and know
> that I am God."*
> —*Psalm 46:10*

It takes about forty minutes to drive from my home on campus to downtown Los Angeles via Pacific Coast highway and the Santa Monica freeway. When we first moved to California, I resented the hours spent in travel, but we soon learned how to use freeway time for family conversation or listening to the Bible on tape which I keep in the car, or to taped lectures and music. When I'm alone in the car, I enjoy singing the prayer songs I love: "Be with Me, Lord," "Be Still, My Soul," "Joyful, Joyful, We Adore Thee," "Take My Life and Let It Be." There is time, too, to pray for each member of my family, time to worship God.

It's easy to become so occupied with our scheduled activities—work, home, family, church, friends, and community service—that we run constantly without stopping to think about it. We're like the football player with fourth down and goal to go. The pressure is on. We want to grab that ball and score. But the coach calls for a time-out. Why? Because we need to think about what we're doing.

God is our coach, and he knows that the more pressure we're under, the more important our tasks, the more we need time out.

Surprisingly, Elton Trueblood, in *The Company of the Committed*, suggests that "one of the best secrets of the discipline of time is the fuller date book." Fill in the empty spaces on your calendar with important commitments—meditation, solitude, prayer, reading, family.

We need to stop from time to time, to look out and see the people around us, to look down and see the flowers, to look up and commune with God.

Take Time for God

The average adult spends a third of her life sleeping. Of the remaining 113 hours a week, 50 are spent on discretionary activities—the things she chooses to do with her time. This adds up to over two thousand hours a year, one thousand hours more than her grandparents had. Between the ages of sixteen and sixty-eight, those hours are the equivalent of eleven years.

Approximately four-fifths of our discretionary time is spent on the media—TV and radio, newspapers and magazines, records, tapes and movies.

In a seventy-year life span, according to one source, approximately three years are spent on education, eight on amusements, four in conversation, and fourteen reading. But in the same time period, even if a woman goes to church every week and spends five minutes each morning and evening in prayer, she will total only five months with God.

When God created the world, he rested on the seventh day, and he commanded a Sabbath day of rest for the Jews. Even though we are no longer under the law of Moses, what if we devoted one day each week to worship, family enjoyment, rest, and meditation? We'd have to prepare for it in advance and guard it jealously.

I'm not talking about that day you're going to take off when you've finished everything that needs to be done. That day will never come. As Gordon MacDonald said, "We do not rest because our work is done; we rest because God commanded it and created us to have a need for it." It's one of his blessings to be accepted without guilt. As Jesus said, "The Sabbath was made for man, not man for the Sabbath" (Mark 2:27).

Our minds and bodies operate at peak strength on Monday. After sleeping Monday night, most, but not all, of our energy is restored. Through the rest of the week, however, our strength gradually wanes until we hit bottom on Saturday night. If we take Sunday as a day of worship and rest, we can regain full vigor for the week ahead.

Ministers may need Monday as a Sabbath since Sunday is a workday for them. Working women who use Saturday to clean house, shop, and catch up need Sunday for rest. Silence, light meals, walks, prayers, and play should be considered.

God doesn't give us the solution to our too-busy lives. He *is* the solution. As Jesus said, "Come to me, all you who are weary and burdened, and I will give you rest" (Matt. 11:28). As the familiar hymn puts it, "Art thou weary, art thou languid, Art thou sore distressed? 'Come to Me,' saith One, 'and coming, be at rest.'" Or, as Augustine said, "Thou hast created us for thyself, and our heart cannot be quieted till it may find repose in thee." Divine communion is at the core of the Christian life.

As a wheel spins at the outside but remains still at the hub because the axle gives it stability, our lives can be very busy on the outside while maintaining serenity at the center. A wheel that goes spinning off its axle becomes useless and destructive. So do our lives, if we fail to center them on God.

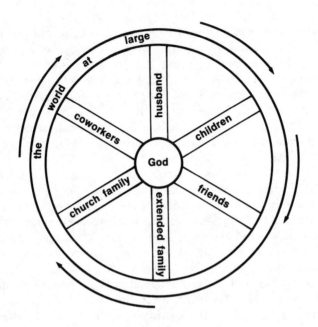

Malcolm Muggeridge noted that, when God appeared to Elijah, it was "not in the wind that rent the mountains and broke in pieces the rocks; not in the earthquake that followed, nor in the fire that followed the earthquake. In a still small voice. Not in the screeching of tires, either, or in the grinding of brakes; not in the roar of the jets or the whistle of sirens; not in the howl of trombones, the rattle of drums or the chanting of demo voices. Again, that still, small voice—if only one could catch it."

How do we catch God's voice? By being still—slowing down, quieting ourselves—and listening. "Be still, and know that I am God" (Ps. 46:10).

In our communication-oriented age, we have grown leery of silence. If someone is around, we have to keep talking, even if we have nothing to say. When we are by ourselves, we turn on the TV or radio. Even in our worship services we seem to be afraid of "dead air" time. The hour becomes so packed with songs, prayers, Scriptures, and sermons that we have no time to meditate. Such a lifestyle promotes hurried and superficial contacts with God, with others, and with our own inner selves.

Even our religious activities can get in the way. We can be too busy doing things for God to spend time with him. He doesn't need our frantic efforts. He wants us. What about the times we rush to church, then home to fix a big dinner? Do we stop long enough to catch our breath and think about what we're doing? It takes time to truly worship God—to praise him and open our heart to his message. It takes leisure for a profound worship experience.

Plans for Making Sunday Special

1. Ask for the cooperation of the family.
2. Prepare meal for Sunday noon on Saturday.
3. Do not stay out late on Saturday night.
4. Plan, prepare, and lay out Sunday's clothes for each member of the family on Saturday night.
5. Have a simple breakfast.
6. Leave a ten-minute time cushion.
7. Plan to arrive at the church building early.

We should spend some time each day in quiet time or devotional study. Milton Jones explains that when inquirers have come to him with spiritual problems, he used to ask, "How's your quiet time?" Now he asks, "When did you stop having one? Have you ever met a mature Christian who continually neglected prayer and Bible study?"

We need time to read God's Word. *Power for Today* and other devotional guides include Scriptures, short commentaries or illustrations, a sentence prayer and a suggested song on a given theme. Or we can plan our own study. God speaks to us through his Word. We need to read it carefully and meditatively, with a notebook handy to jot down thoughts and questions.

Psychiatrist Paul Meier writes of the importance of meditating on the Scriptures to promote mental health. According to Meier, we are holistic people. Each aspect of our nature affects our entire being. God's thought patterns and values are in

Some How-To's for Devotions

I. *Prayer*
   Keep a prayer list.
   Bracket your study time with prayer.
   Balance petitions with praise and thanksgiving.
   Listen.

II. *Study*
   Read a book of the Bible through at one sitting.
   Read one chapter, thinking about its implications for you.
   Read a verse and look up chain references.
   Look up references to one word in a concordance.
   Use a prepared devotional guide.
   Read a chapter of a devotional book.

III. *Meditation*
   Take notes on your reading.
   Pause and let the message sink in.
   Determine one concrete step to take to apply what
      you've learned.

contrast to our own. As we meditate on them, we become more calm and rational.

We need time to pray. "I'm so busy, I just don't have time to pray," someone says. "Well, I'm too busy not to," her wiser friend replies. Prayer is our response to God. We need to retreat from the demands of life occasionally, as Jesus did. "After he had dismissed [the crowd], he went up on a mountainside by himself to pray" (Matt. 14:23 RSV).

My friend Betty is a woman of prayer. She prays on her way to work each morning—a forty-minute commute. She prays for her family as they go to work and to class. She prays for the church and the particular needs of individual Christians. She prays over problems she'll meet on the job. After she gets to work, she prays before dealing with difficult customers and employees. The time she spends with God can be seen in her personal poise and in her relationships with family and friends, customers and coworkers.

We need time to sing songs of praise and to memorize Scriptures. One young mother posts a different Scripture verse each day above the table where she changes her baby's diaper. By the end of the day, she has memorized it.

We need time to examine ourselves and to confess our sins. Guilt is a mental depressant which enervates and burdens us.

We need time to sharpen our axes, to prepare for our ministry. Moses spent forty years in the desert. Paul went into Arabia before he started his great work. Jesus' life was made up of ten years of silence for each year of ministry.

We need time to practice the presence of Christ, to focus on him. We live on two levels at once—the level of divine communion and the level of the physical world. We cannot shine for the Lord unless we are plugged into the proper power source. We may get so tied up with our activities that we confuse our value with what we do. God knows our hearts. He is more interested in what we *are* than in what we *do*.

Hints for a Richer Devotional Life

Dear God, I want my prayer life to be richer. Help me overcome

1. distractions
2. intrusions into my quiet time
3. lack of faith
4. noise

This week I will write out my prayer and concentrate on:
Monday—adoration
Tuesday—confession
Wednesday—thanksgiving
Thursday—supplication or intercession for missionaries
Friday—supplication or intercession for the sick
Saturday—supplication or intercession for my family
Sunday—supplication or intercession for the church

I will make a prayer list of ten people whom I most want to pray for and use this list each day in intercessory prayer.

The devotional book I plan to read in the next year is:

To increase my devotional life I will begin keeping a journal of my thoughts and prayers, longings and problems.

Take Time to Rejuvenate

It doesn't take experts to tell us that we are suffering from the "universal fatigue" of time pressure and the pace of life.

Even some of our leisure activities—such as packaged tours and organized athletics—merely add to our emphasis on scheduling and time. But there are activities that help us relax:

1. Getting Away

Gordon, our former minister, tells of going with five other men on a three-day pack horse trip to a high mountain lake in the sawtooth range of Idaho. "We fished, slept, ate and marveled at the wonders of God's majestic mountains, blue lakes, crystal streams, and flower-covered high mountains. We sat around a campfire and discussed the Bible, laughed at everything and nothing. No phones ringing, no television, no roar of traffic, no smog, no human problems crying out for solution.

"When we had almost reached the valley on our return, we began to hear the roar of motorcycles, the blare of radios, the strident cries of the human species. 'We have returned to civilization,' one of the men remarked."

The pace, noise, crowds and deadlines of our daily lives put stress on our bodies, minds, and souls. We have more time for leisure than ever before, but so often our leisure activities are anything but relaxing. A friend of mine is constantly "getting away" for long weekends. She drives great distances, returning late and tired with frayed nerves and dirty clothes, having to be at work the next morning. Her vacations often are more exhausting than relaxing.

2. Positive Thinking

Tension comes from a sense of urgency that makes us feel rushed even when we aren't. As William James said, "Neither the nature nor the amount of our work is accountable for the frequency and severity of our breakdowns. Their cause lies, rather, in the absurd feeling of hurry and having no time, in breathlessness, tension and anxiety."

Rushing was a habit with me. I noticed, for instance, that I was changing lanes repeatedly on the freeway just to get one car length ahead, even when I had plenty of time to get where I was going. When I started consciously to relax, I noticed that, if I made the lane change, the car I had been following often reached the exit at about the same time I did. I wasn't gaining much by these automotive maneuvers, and I was wearing myself out.

When we feel hurried, fearful, resentful, or worried, it makes us tired. We need to think thoughts of hope, confidence, and goodwill. "Whatever is . . . excellent or praiseworthy—think about such things" (Phil. 4:8).

3. Rest

The prolific writer Ray Bradbury works on three to four projects a week—screenplays, novels, short stories, essays, book reviews, poems. Where does he get the energy?

"I hoard energy," he says. "I do my important writing in the morning. When the energy begins to disappear I take care of mail and run errands. Around three in the afternoon I take a nap. I've been doing that every day since I was fifteen. That brings all my energy back and the juices begin flowing again. After that it's usually a quiet evening at home. We don't go out much."

Those who never let go cannot hang on. Sometimes we master the skills of activity but not of serenity. It is as important to know how to rest as to know how to work. Rest doesn't diminish what we do, but frees us from tension so we can accomplish more. It helps us recuperate from the work we've already done and strengthens us for more effective and dynamic service.

Karl Barth points out the need to consider rest in formulating church activities and statements. "If we were to do this," he says, "we might then work much more earnestly and productively and in a manner far more impressively Christian."

A good example of the problem is Jean Fleming's story of neighbors who had been attracted to Christ but felt from her example that they "couldn't be Christians; we couldn't live at your pace." She admits, "The busyness of our lives intimidated them, and they put off making a commitment because of it."

Some people say, "I don't have time to rest. I have too much to do." But at what cost? Irritability, loss of efficiency, overpowering fatigue? Jesus knew his disciples needed rest. "Come with me by yourselves to a quiet place, and get some rest," he told them (Mark 6:31). We need to spend time on ourselves—to recharge and rejuvenate.

Some people feel guilty when they relax. But relaxation is not a sin. It is a necessary balance to the activities of life. When you work, work hard and accomplish as much as possible. When you stop, stop.

4. Sleep

We all need sleep to repair our bodies, relax our minds, and release our emotions. Brainwashing generally involves sleep deprivation, because people break under the strain of sleeplessness. Most of us can get by on five or six hours a night, but studies have shown that, on the average, we maintain our greatest efficiency with eight.

Recent research on sleep indicates that it is of two levels: REM or rapid eye movement is the level at which we dream, but delta stage is a deeper and more restorative level. Delta stage sleep is most effective in the hours before midnight, and people who are deprived of it are prone to depression.

You sleep better if you exercise in the morning, avoid caffeine in the afternoon, and get to bed at a regular time. When you go to bed, drop all thoughts of work. If you can't sleep, review the previous day, schedule the coming one, read or pray. Don't worry if you can't get to sleep. Worry keeps you awake.

When the pioneer preacher T.B. Larimore got off a Pullman car to hold a meeting, he was approached by an elder who felt he should have traveled coach. "Brother Larimore, you're wasting the Lord's money," the elder said. "No," Larimore replied, "I'm taking care of the Lord's servant."

5. Good Health Care

How often do we feel we have to keep going only to find we can't? At the first symptom of disease, sleep more, eat better, see a doctor if necessary and listen to her advice.

Preventive medicine can help keep us from becoming ill. Norvel and I are health enthusiasts. We work to eliminate as much salt, fat, sugar, and red meat as possible from our diet. We eat whole grains, fresh fruits and vegetables, chicken and fish. We take our vitamins and drink eight glasses of water a day. We know from a health standpoint that we are what we eat.

But we also know that we will not be healthy if we don't exercise. So every morning we put on our jogging suits, go to the university track, and walk two miles before breakfast.

Exercise is essential—especially for those of us with desk jobs. The premature death rate is six times higher for sedentary professionals than for farmers and miners. Even the early Greeks knew that the body influences the mind. Exercise increases self-esteem, relieves anxiety, improves attentiveness, dissipates stress, and elevates the mood, according to Roy J. Shepherd, director of the School of Physical and Health Education at the University of Toronto.

The amount of exercise we need depends on our purpose in doing it. When we exercise to lose weight, we need at least thirty minutes a day. Cardiovascular fitness demands three to five sessions a week of fifteen to sixty minutes each. Stress reduction calls for four to five thirty-minute sessions a week. Just twenty minutes a day four times a week builds muscle.

Get in tune with your inner pacemaker. For the Christian, that pacemaker is God. As Toki Miyashina wrote:

> The Lord is my Pace-setter: I shall not rush. He makes me stop and rest for quiet intervals; he provides me with images of stillness, which restore my serenity. He leads me in ways of efficiency through great calmness of mind; and his guidance is peace. Even though I have a great many things to accomplish each day, I will not fret, for his presence is here. His timeliness, his all-importance will keep me in balance. He prepares refreshment and renewal in the midst of my activity by anointing my mind with his oils of tranquility. My cup of joyous energy overflows. Surely harmony and effectiveness shall be the fruits of all my hours, for I shall walk in the pace of my Lord, and dwell in his house forever.

Take Time to Think Creatively

I have had an hourglass for years. It is really a twenty-minute glass—pink sand encased in a clear plastic cube. It is fascinating to watch the smooth trickle of sand flow swiftly through the neck of the glass as I time a phone call or a "quicky" project. From the hourglass we get the picturesque phrases "the sands of time" and "time is running out." Sometimes I wonder if people appreciated time more when hourglasses were used than they do now with digital watches and solid state clocks.

But time passes at the same rate no matter how it is measured. Yet as precious as time is, there are those moments when we need to go slowly and deliberately—when someone dear needs us, when a great decision is to be made, when we are tempted to be judgmental or react in anger.

When we don't give time to thought, our efforts will be half-baked and rushed. According to Robert Banks, "It is only when we cease our restless doing that we will discover what needs to be done."

Though most of us say we believe in education, few of us spend much time thinking. In our culture some people are paid to think, but all of us need to do more of it.

Thinking is best done in private. If you can't find privacy to think, make it by getting up early or staying up late. Discipline your mind to think without jumping up to do things. Reading the Bible or great books of literature, philosophy, theology, or devotion can help.

Thinking takes time. What if we turned down appointments and blocked off time on our calendars to think? We wouldn't dream of interrupting someone who was talking, but what about those who are busy thinking? We rob ourselves of creative solutions by underestimating the importance of thought. As Banks points out, "Innovations in science, in art, and in other spheres surface when mind and spirit are relaxed and open to the subconscious." Ruskin said, "There is no music in a rest, but there's the making of music in it." And Georgia O'Keeffe pointed out, "Still—in a way—nobody sees a flower—really it is so small—we haven't time—and to see takes time, like to have a friend takes time."

Reading stimulates thought. Take time to read. Keep books by your bedside and read for a few minutes before you go to sleep. Keep them on the coffee table or in your purse or briefcase for reading during coffee breaks. And when you're on your way to the car, pick up a book for reading during unexpected waits.

One year when my children were little, I realized that I hadn't read much since graduating from college. I determined that, despite two preschoolers, I would read twelve books that year—one a month. I read twenty-six that year, and have read thirty to forty every year since!

Peg Bracken, author of the *I Hate To Cook Book*, gives six commandments for women, including "Thou shalt periodically clean out your mental closets to make room for new merchandise." What new things have you learned this year? this month? this week? today?

My friend Elsie decided she wanted to go back to school for her master's degree. Since she works during the day as a speech therapist for the local schools, she would have to take night classes. She almost gave up when she discovered that it would take six years to complete the program, but a coworker put it in a different light. "The six years will pass any way," she said, "whether you have your master's degree at the end of it or not."

Be selective. Spend your leisure time in a variety of challenging, satisfying, enriching activities which help you grow, keep you from getting stale, and fit your stage of life. Be adventurous. Live!

Take Time to Love

"Everybody needs at least three hugs a day in order to be healthy," says Professor Sidney B. Simon of the University of Massachusetts at Amherst. Simon points out that children with Down's syndrome walk earlier if they are hugged, touched, and stroked. The heartbeat of patients in intensive care units stabilizes more quickly when nurses hold their hands. Students hugged at home get higher grades.

It takes time to love. It takes time to care for others, cherish them, take responsibility for their well-being and happiness. It takes time to kiss your husband good-bye, to laugh with your friend, to share a gentle word or a sincere compliment, to listen, to send a thoughtful note or a simple gift. A life that is too busy for love is too busy.

I spend a lot of time with my son Robert when we're driving together. When I'm on campus at Pepperdine for work or other events, I like to meet my daughter Kathy for lunch. I've always involved both of them in my work—discussing problems and soliciting suggestions.

One day on our way to lectureship, I asked Robert to take down some of my ideas for future issues of *20th Century Christian*. Then I asked if he had any of his own. "Why don't you do something about kids?" he said. "You know, it's tough to be a kid." That phrase became the theme of one of the next year's issues, and he wrote an article for it.

Laziness is a sin, but so is too-busy-ness. When we neglect our families, ignore our brothers and sisters, and alienate our non-Christian friends, we aren't doing God's will no matter what we spend our time doing. We need to schedule time for our families and friends—even if we have to put it on our calendars far in advance.

Keith Miller tells the story of a busy business executive rushing to catch a train in an eastern city. He had given up trying to live a "personal" daily life because of the great demands on his time. As he rushed to the train he promised himself that he would try to be a real Christian that morning instead of just talking about it. He was late, and as he rushed across the lobby, hearing the last "all aboard," he bumped into a small child carrying a new jigsaw puzzle. The pieces flew across the platform. The executive paused, saw the boy in tears, and with a sigh, stopped, stooped down, and began to help pick up the pieces as the train pulled out. When they finished, the little boy looked up in awe. "Mister," he said hesitantly, "are you Jesus?" And the man realized that, at least for one moment that morning, he had been.

Those of us with children need to take time to make memories with them. We give our time to the things we value. What does it profit a woman if she gains a million dollars and loses her own child?

Time with family is easily put off for the urgent matters that crowd our days. We need to schedule some time together every day. It takes time to keep our marriages holy, healthy, and happy. To share our feelings, work through problems, do those little things that let our husbands know we care.

We can become so efficient—working all the time, making each minute count—that we turn into machines. I remember rushing in from a conference on Saturday to find a plate, cat food, and a can opener on the front porch. Our neighbor had put it there so we would feed the cats, but no one had been outside to see it. My car was loaded with a week's worth of dirty clothes, plans for the magazine, reports from our booth, and expense records. My husband met me at the door with a big kiss, but my mind was so full of cat food and dirty clothes and work I could hardly kiss him back.

Phyllis Martens wrote, "A vital aspect of love is that parents give of themselves—spelled TIME. Nothing, not the most glittering gift from Santa-Claus-land, can take the place of Mom reading stories to the little ones and Dad discussing his son's dating problems with him."

We need to take time for relaxed family meals, to oversee homework, to talk with our children about their day at school. We need to talk and plan, to create traditions, celebrate holidays and birthdays, take family trips. It isn't the money spent but the magic of the time together.

Skip a few vacations and share the money you'd spend with someone who needs it. Spend the time resting, studying, teaching vacation Bible school, planting a garden, working on the house, learning a craft or musical instrument. My friend Sheila and her family have spent several summer vacations teaching vacation Bible school on an Indian reservation in Arizona.

What about a backyard vacation? Pitch a tent. Have picnics in the yard or at a park or the beach. Have candlelight dinners at home or in interesting new restaurants. Participate in sports, visit museums, art galleries, and zoos. Visit courtrooms, fire stations, newspaper offices, and TV stations. Be creative. Memories don't have to be expensive.

Take time for parents. Go out to lunch together, write or call if they live far away, send pictures and clippings and other things they'll appreciate.

We need to take time for a ministry to others—to help, to be a friend, to share our faith. We can participate in events that bring people together—courses at a community college, concerts, and aerobics classes. We can have people over for meals or special movies on the VCR or singalongs. We can look in on elderly neighbors or work as volunteers.

Give at least one "cup of cold water" every day—a phone call or post card, a visit to a hospital or nursing home, preparing food, or helping meet some other need.

Take time to speak to strangers—the checker in the grocery store, the waitress at the restaurant, the attendant at the gas station. Call them by name. Ask questions that will help you get to know them. It takes less than a minute. Keith Miller calls it a "thirty-second island of caring."

Leo F. Buscaglia wrote, "We must never underestimate the power of a single glance or encouraging word. A smile can make someone's day. One small expression of caring has the potential to turn a life around."

We must take time for God, for ourselves, and for others. If we don't take it voluntarily, all our hurry and stress can make us ill, and we will be forced to take it whether we want to or not. As Patricia Clifford says in her poem "Time,"

> The modern life is
> hurry,
>   scurry,
>   worry;
> No time for lasting, loving relationships;
> No time for caring or sharing,
> No time! Never enough time for
> thinking,
>   reading,
>   praying,
>   loving,
>   caring;
> Never enough time.
>
> Then God intervenes;
> time is granted—
> Though not always welcomed—
> through
>   illness,
>   accident,
>   loss of job,

family crisis;
Minutes pass unnoticed;
Hours mean nothing.

Oh, the blessedness of time—
Time to contemplate,
  to think
    to be,
      to know,
        to find—
The truth in life,
The good in life,
The real in life
God in life.

Questions and Activities

1. How much time do you spend with God? To your regular worship and devotion times, remember to add the time spent studying for classes. Are you pleased with the total?

2. Do you eat wholesome meals? get plenty of sleep? How about exercise? Study your habits and work out a program to fill the gaps.

3. Choose some field of study you want to learn more about and start a program of reading. Check your local library for a start.

4. How much time do you spend with others—your family, friends, and those who need you? Plan to spend some time with each member of your family and make special contact with at least one other person a day.

5. Fill out a wheel chart like the one described previously.

9
Time at Home

"Train the younger women to love their husbands and children, to be self-controlled and pure, to be busy at home."
—Titus 2:4

I have always admired efficiency. As a preacher's wife and the mother of four, I began early to list time-savers and clip articles on time management in the home.

My mother taught school when I was young, and though she took me to school with her and I learned a great deal, I didn't learn much about homemaking. My sister Kathryn was in charge of the house, and my brothers and I were supposed to keep our own rooms, but I was negligent.

When Norvel and I married, someone asked Mother, "Can she cook?"

"No," she said, "but she can read." I had a lot of good cookbooks, and Mother felt I could learn to cook on my own.

But I wanted my daughters to learn early to be efficient homemakers, so we formed a girls' club. Once a week, eleven girls from seven to twelve years of age met at our house after school. Various mothers would take turns teaching them to make donuts, knit, and weave potholders. We even practiced vacuuming. We felt that, if they knew how to do household tasks well, they could do them faster and with more enjoyment.

Time spent at home is the least structured time of all. There are many jobs crying to be done—sewing, gardening, cooking, chauffeuring children, refinishing furniture, grooming, plumbing, cleaning, car work, hauling trash, painting—and no one to tell us what to do when.

Physician Walter E. O'Donnel concluded that emotional

Workaholism at Home

Full-time homemakers are often workaholics because there is always something which needs to be done in a home, and there is no employer to say, "That is enough." Check yourself.

	Yes	No
A. I find it very difficult to do nothing.		
B. When the family is having a relaxing time I take along work to do.		
C. I find myself telling others the number of hours I work.		
D. I find it difficult to listen to family members and give them my complete attention because I'm always occupied with some task.		
E. On a vacation I am thinking how much I have to do when I return home.		
F. My life is balanced between work, play, family, church.		

fatigue is more common among women than men because men's work lives are more structured, while women's work at home may seem aimless. It is fatiguing to meet a day filled with so much to do without a plan for doing it.

Home is a workplace, but it is also a place for relationships. Part of our challenge as homemakers is to keep the two in some kind of balance. "Women are the ones who tend to hold together households," says UCLA researcher Dr. Michael Gottlieb. A woman sets the tone of the home—whether it is calm or hectic, somber or happy.

The home of total spontaneity—where two socks that match are seldom clean at once, where there is nothing to eat and nothing clean to eat it on, where you can't sit down without moving something—is obviously a mess. But so is the rigidly organized home—though it dispenses a seemingly endless supply of matching socks, well-balanced meals, and clean surfaces—if it seems sterile and lacking in warmth. The ideal home blends warmth and organization.

Home Is for Loving

James Dobson, in his book *What Wives Wish Their Husbands Knew about Women*, gives the results of his survey of women 25 to 40 who were asked to rank ten major frustrations in their lives in order of their impact. By far the largest percentage placed low self-esteem at the head of the list. Much of our problem with self-esteem results from the multiplicity of demands, both real and imagined—to keep a beautiful house, to look like a *Vogue* model, to be a competent business manager, to be a scintillating companion to our husbands, and to rear outstanding children.

No wonder we feel like failures when our homes are a mess, our children irritable and demanding, our husbands critical and unappreciative, and ourselves constantly fatigued.

What can help? Realistic expectations, for one thing. Understanding and appreciative husbands, surely. But also the realization that this is a special time. That it will not last forever. That our primary responsibility at home is not to cook and clean but to create an environment of love and care for our families.

Even love takes organization. Plan your mornings to allow time for good-bye kisses and loving words at the door. Don't send children out to face the world with rebukes ringing in their ears. If you drop them off on your way to work, make time for a relaxed drive, even if you have to get up a little earlier or stay up a little later to get things ready the night before.

Plan evenings so you can all sit down to dinner together. Time at the table can be a rewarding time of sharing, loving, and expressing interest in each others' activities.

Bedtime, as well, can be special. With forethought, children can be readied for bed without hassles and threats. Take a few minutes for a special family bedtime ritual. When our children were younger, we prayed together and did our own special hug-kiss-and-love routine each night.

Mothers are architects of memories for children. Time is a precious ingredient in these memories. Think carefully before sending your son or daughter to an expensive summer camp. You could take a week off to build a playhouse or plant a garden or work together to help the needy.

Since we have two children, we like to split up, with one of us taking the children and the other getting some choice rest or work time. Or we split up the children and let each enjoy an outing with one parent, switching off the next time. Steven alternates each Saturday, taking a different one of his three children to the restaurant of his or her choice for breakfast.

Six Super Starters for a Super Day

1. Get dressed and put on make-up. You will feel better all day.
2. Fix breakfast. Set the table the night before if possible. Wash dishes or put in dishwasher after you eat.
3. Decide on menu for dinner and begin preparations (take meat from freezer, etc.).
4. Make beds.
5. Walk through the house and pick up. Do not spend more than five minutes in a room. Use a laundry basket to retrieve misplaced items.
6. Take seven minutes to read the Bible and pray.

If possible, don't go out the front door until you've finished the Super Starters. If you have to eliminate some, at least dress, make the bed, and set the table.

Give yourself grace time. If you have been up all night with a sick child and are emotionally and physically exhausted, treat yourself with the fruit of the Spirit—patience, kindness, goodness. This is the way God treats you. Then start fresh the next day.

Don't forget that each member of the family needs some time alone—for creative activity, thinking, or daydreaming, for recharging after the demands of the day, for prayer and meditation.

Spend time teaching your children—about God, the world, art, literature, and music. Teach them to enjoy reading by reading to them—and by reading yourself. Teach them to make choices by giving them choices to make. Even very young children can choose between two acceptable outfits to wear or two fillings for a sandwich. Teach them to make decisions, to develop their own tastes, to get in touch with themselves. It is part of becoming an independent adult.

Delegation is a part of good time management. Jesus probably asked the women who traveled with him to arrange his housing, food, and clothing, as well as to help his ministry in other ways. He sent the disciples into the town of Sychar while he rested by the well. He instructed the servants to fill the water pots at the wedding feast at Cana.

My sister Kathryn feels that her role as a mother is not to do for her children what they can do for themselves. The goal of a mother is to make the child independent of her. So delegation is not only good for your schedule but good for your children. And work comes in all sizes. An eighteen-month-old can bring you a book. A two-year-old can empty the wastebasket. A three-year-old can set the table.

The job of a mother is to work herself out of a job. The average woman will have some thirty years after her children are grown. Plan for the end of your child-rearing years. Plan for the empty nest. Develop outside interests and activities. Prepare for a career if you don't have one, or decide to devote more time and energy to the career you have.

You and your husband need time alone together, to strengthen your relationship for the day when it's "just the two of you" again. Slip away to a cozy restaurant occasionally. An overnighter, even in a local hotel, can make you feel like newlyweds. Show love in little ways each day.

The woman who lives alone should realize that her home can be a place for loving as well. It can be a place for entertaining, counseling, encouraging, and sharing happy times—not just a place to display possessions or to camp out.

Keeping your home relatively clean and tidy and giving thought to decorating details will make it more attractive for yourself and for others. Your home should reflect your personality—your warmth or whimsy, your interests and concerns.

Home Is for Work

It takes a lot of effort to maintain a comfortable environment. Whether we have jobs outside the home or are full-time homemakers, we have many of the same tasks to fit into our schedules. Our attitude toward our work makes all the difference.

I can mop the bathroom floor and resent every minute of it because I am thinking, "Here I am with a college education—I was meant for greater things than this." Or I can say, "How wonderful to have a bathroom, when nine-tenths of the women in the world don't have one. Isn't it great to be able to mop a floor, to see it shine, to get it clean for the people I love? I do this gladly to keep my family healthy and give them an attractive place to live."

According to Tony Campolo, "No woman should be conned into feeling that being a homemaker is a worthless and inferior vocation. While some women find that this vocation holds little emotional fulfillment, . . . for many women, keeping a house and caring for children is a full-time job and provides all the emotional gratification they could ever hope to have. . . . While a woman should not feel obligated to be a full-time homemaker simply by virtue of her sexual identity, she should feel free to deliberately choose this role if she believes it to be the vocation to which God has called her."

We may be tempted to feel that, if we didn't have a house to keep or children to rear, we could do something for the Lord. But a Christian is a Christian seven days a week. As we do our work at home, we are serving others and glorifying God.

Cleaning

It is easier to get things done with a plan. Have a regular cleaning schedule. Most of us who work during the week clean house on Saturdays. Those who are at home can take a room a day. Housekeeping should be a family affair. All the routine maintenance tasks should not automatically fall to the mother. Here are some practical suggestions for speeding your cleaning tasks:

1. Start early and do the difficult jobs first. Learn the difference between fatigue and laziness. Study your energy levels to determine your prime and low times of the day. Schedule demanding tasks for prime times, routine for low.
2. Have jobs at hand for "down time." One woman made her living room curtains while talking on the phone. She got a headset from the telephone company, and only worked on the curtains when the phone rang, leaving them when the conversation was over.
3. Spread major jobs through the year—one a month.

House Cleaning Schedule

Once a week:

1. change sheets
2. do laundry
3. plan menus
4. buy groceries
5. vacuum carpets
6. mop floors
7. dust and polish furniture
8. clean bathrooms
9. clean stove and refrigerator

Once or twice a year:

1. clean carpets
2. wash woodwork and windows
3. launder bedspreads, blankets, curtains
4. clean garage
5. store out-of-season clothes
6. polish silver

4. Cut down on cleaning time and stop wasting time looking for things by keeping kitchen and work areas

neat and well organized. Have a place for everything and keep everything in its place—the logical place—as near the location where you will be using it as possible.

5. Shop for drawer and houseware organizers. Put away your materials when you finish work on a project for the day.

6. Take "out-of-place" items with you when you leave a room. If you have a two-story house, keep a basket on the landing for items to go up or down.

7. Put away clean dishes before you start a meal. If you have a dishwasher, add to it until you have a load, then run it all at once. If you wash dishes by hand, don't dry them; scald them and let them drain dry. Clean sink, counters, and range each time you do dishes.

8. Use paper plates occasionally. Do quick cleanups with paper towels and tissue; cook in aluminum foil to save pans. Carry a sack from room to room to empty trash baskets; then make only one trip to the central dumping place.

9. Keep clutter off the floor for both appearance and safety. When my children were small, I worked with them to pick up toys twice a day—at naptime and bedtime.

10. Do things only as well as they need to be done. If you're a concert pianist, put more effort into your playing than into washing the car. There are four ways to dust furniture: (1) dust everything thoroughly, (2) dust only the top which shows, (3) pull the blinds, or (4) write "welcome" in the dust.

One woman tells how she tried to put her house in "dying condition" at night. Before going to bed every night, she would walk through the house and put things away. Then, if she died before morning, there wouldn't be a mess for people to see!

Room for Improvement

1. Start housecleaning at the entrance to your home. Clean the entrance area, then the rooms a guest would be most likely to see. Don't forget

that your family members are the most important people who enter your home.

2. Clean as you go. As you leave a room, see that it is as straight as when you entered. Wipe off the bathroom sink and mirror after use. When cooking, place utensils in a sink of soapy water after use.

3. Pick up before bedtime. Every good morning starts the night before.

4. To help children learn to clean their room, put everything that is out of place on the bed and have them start from there.

5. Have a schedule for food preparation. Plan menus a week ahead.

6. Have two add-to lists, one for errands and another for groceries, so one trip a week will suffice. (There will be exceptions for unexpected guests and emergencies.)

7. Add "divine interruptions" to the schedule for the day. Expect the unexpected. Plan, but be flexible.

Food Preparation

The following suggestions will help you prepare varied and wholesome meals for your family in very little time:

1. Start your main dish, make a salad and chill, cook vegetables, then heat bread. Have bowls and serving utensils out and ready to fill in order to get everything to the table at once.

2. Freeze leftovers into TV dinner trays or use in soups and stews. Cook food in the dish in which it will be served. Use a crockpot or microwave.

3. Prepare food in advance, especially for company dinners. Double cook potatoes, rice, casseroles, spaghetti sauce, meats, and poultry.

4. Peel vegetables on paper towels or newspapers. Line the broiler with aluminum foil and the kitchen trash with a grocery sack or plastic bag.

5. Mix pancake batter in a large measuring cup and pour onto the griddle.

6. Set a timer so you won't have to watch the clock.

7. Arrange cupboards with the most often-used items in easiest reach. Have spoons and scoops in flour, sugar,

and other items which must be measured. Keep spices in alphabetical order.

8. Don't waste time and money on poor equipment. The tools you use most often—knives, scissors, can opener—should be sturdy and well-made. Use the best tool for the job. Portable chopping blocks, tongs, wire whisks, potato peelers, and flexible metal spatulas are great timesaving tools, but remember to clean wooden chopping blocks immediately after use and bleach occasionally.

9. Plan menus in advance. Keep a supply of quick-to-prepare food. Try not to shop more often than once a week, looking ahead for company meals, potlucks, and parties.

10. Keep a running list of things you need for all family members to add to. Add specials from newspaper, items from coupons (including size and style), and whatever you need to fill out menus for the week.

Clothes

Here are some suggestions for the purchase and upkeep of clothes:

1. Find a good schedule for washing, which keeps everyone in clothes, and stick to it. You may have to wash more often if you dry clothes on the line.

2. Fold clothes immediately and stack each person's things separately.

3. As the children grow and sizes are harder to distinguish, buy distinctive colors or styles of underwear for individual family members. Buy men's socks of the same brand in only two basic colors, so it's easier to match pairs.

4. Each family member should put away his own clean clothes and put his dirty ones in the hamper. No one should have to search through the house at wash time.

5. Iron as little as possible. Do a few pieces in the evening in front of a favorite TV program.

Margie, my schoolteacher friend, prepares five outfits each

weekend for her son Brian. She hangs them together in his closet so he has matched outfits for each day of the week with minimum hassle in the mornings.

Household Business

The following suggestions will help make varied household tasks easier:

1. Make a list and run all your errands at once. Plot your stops to make each trip a circle. If possible, hit freeways and stores at non-peak hours.
2. Plan on the run. Have a pen and note pad in your purse to organize and make lists while waiting in the doctor's office or for the kids at school.
3. Use the phone to shop for sheets and things you don't have to see to buy. Also remember to "let your fingers do the walking" by phoning, not driving, around to locate items.
4. Keep duplicates in rooms where they are used often—especially scissors, note pads, and pens. Keep a note pad and pen by the bed to jot down those late-night inspirations.
5. Set two days a month to pay bills—early enough so none of the payments will be late.
6. Mark birthdays and anniversaries on your calendar and keep a supply of cards on hand.
7. Group phone calls and correspondence. Use a long phone cord or portable phone so you can work as you talk. Have something useful to do when you're "on hold." Set a kitchen timer when you have to "call back in half an hour."

We leave phone messages, as well as other notes to family members, at their places at the table. Everyone knows where to look, and messages don't get misplaced.

Recycling is one area in which fastest is not best. Keep piles of newspapers and sacks of bottles and cans to take to the recycling center. Even if you don't collect money for them, we all benefit from preserving our natural resources.

A woman who manages an apartment building found a man going through their trash cans for items to recycle. She asked him to come by on a regular basis, then set up separate bins for papers, bottles, and cans. The residents had the satisfaction of doing something worthwhile, and the man got the money for taking the things to the recycling center.

Home Is for Hospitality

Karen Mains, in *Open Heart, Open Home*, makes an important distinction between entertaining, which involves impressing people, and hospitality, which is a part of our Christian service.

Our attitude toward hospitality rubs off on our children, our husbands, and our guests. If we are hurried and harried, everyone will suffer. Most of us could probably use less energy in preparation and have more for enjoying a relaxed visit.

If you're having guests for dinner, plan simple appetizers of cheese, crackers, and fruit juice to nibble on while you start the main dish. It also reduces tensions and the chance of ruined dishes if your guests are delayed.

Be prepared for unexpected company by making double batches of freezable main dishes and desserts. One woman often cooks for her family and another family on Sunday. She then is prepared to invite visitors home from church.

Consider the advantages of having guests for dinner two nights in a row so you can clean and arrange flowers once for both. How about serving the same menu to different people? It helps you to master the routine, and nobody is the wiser.

Don't hesitate to let your guests help with last-minute preparations and cleanup chores. Some of the best visits occur over the kitchen sink.

Keep spare beds made and ready for use by overnight guests. Spend a night in your guest room to see what supplies would be useful. An alarm clock, books or magazines, a nightlight or flashlight, and trial-sized toiletries are appreciated. Be sure to have extra towels, soap, and bathroom tissue on hand.

Once we had a prominent minister spend two nights in our

guest room while he was lecturing on campus. When he told us good-bye, he thanked us for the wonderful visit. But when I went to his room to change the sheets, I found there were none on the bed. He'd slept on the mattress pad for two nights!

Some mistakes, like this one, are the result of our own negligence. Others are unavoidable disasters. Mike and Marla arrived for dinner with friends to find that a pipe had burst, filling their basement with fifteen feet of water. The woman had set their table with fine china on the lawn. The two couples had a lovely meal, then the men worked together to pump out the water.

Keep a good sense of humor and realize that nothing is perfect in this life.

Home Is for Organization

"Use your head and save your feet," as my teacher used to tell me, and nowhere is the advice more appropriate than in the home. The average housewife walks 1,037 miles a year on her job. How many of those miles could be eliminated with better planning?

Consider the way you use your time at home—the time spent cooking, sewing, mending, and cleaning; the time spent on child care—physical, spiritual, and mental; and the time spent on Bible study, prayer, and church work.

If you're dissatisfied with your current schedule:

1. Admit your need for improvement.
2. Ask God for help.
3. Identify those areas of greatest difficulty.
4. Concentrate on one at a time.
5. List possible ways to improve.
6. Don't work on another item until you're satisfied with the first.

Question the way you do things.
Is this job necessary? Why?
Who should do it? Why?
Where should it be done? Why?
When should it be done? Why?
How should it be done? Why?

Evaluate alternatives. Look for ways to improve the procedure, to omit or combine steps. Your resources for your work at home include money, time, energy, and tools, but they also include brains, imagination, skill, and determination. Put them all to work for you in organizing your time at home.

"Simplify and eliminate," as Anne Ortlund puts it. Most of us have too many things—in our houses and on our minds. A hundred years ago, the average person regarded sixteen items as necessities, with only seventy-two on the average person's "want list." Now we consider ninety-four items necessities and would like to have 484 others!

All these things can get in our way. We need to weed out, throw away, give away. Cut down on do-dads, appliances, utensils, and clothes. Cull closets and kitchen cabinets regularly. Someone suggested boxing up kitchen items and putting them on the back porch, then bringing back items as needed. What's left in the box after a month or so should be tossed or given away. Use three paper bags as you clean—one marked "toss," one "give away," and one "keep." Toss the first, take the second to church or a thrift store, and find the most efficient place to store the items in the third.

Make room for more important things, as this paper I wrote several years ago suggests:

> I've lost it, Lord. Somewhere in all this clutter, I've lost my peace of mind, my sense of direction, my awareness of you. Maybe it's buried under these dirty clothes. Why do we have so many clothes, Lord, when so many people are cold? It may be in that pile of bills on the desk or under the stereo or behind the microwave. Could I retrieve it with a personal computer?
>
> Maybe it's lost in the clutter of my days—dropped down the crack between the 10 A.M. board meeting and my luncheon appointment. Maybe I dropped it as I was hurrying to get out of the car with the groceries and Bobby was already home from school and was crying on the front porch because the door was locked and he didn't know where I was.
>
> However it happened, I lost it, Lord. And suddenly I realize that nothing else really matters. Help me do some spring cleaning, Lord. Help me clear the clutter from my house and my mind and my life. Help me find my sense of your presence once more.

Questions and Activities

1. Complete this sentence: Since I am largely responsible for the atmosphere in my home, for making it a place of love, peace, and security, I will nurture my own relationship with God by:

2. Number in order your priorities as a homemaker: (   ) meals, (   ) children, (   ) beautiful house, (   ) community service, (   ) God, (   ) outside career, (   ) husband, (   ) entertaining, (   ) self, (   ) home maintenance, (   ) yard maintenance, (   ) friends. How would you like them to be ranked?

3. Grade your housekeeping skills on a scale of 1 to 10 (10 being highest):

Skill	Grade
Super starters	
Menu planning	
Shopping	
Delegating to children	
Telephoning	
Devotional life	
Clean as you go	
Meals on time	
Laundry and mending	
Planning for fun	

4. Do my family and friends know when it is convenient for me to talk on the phone? Do I ask, "Is this a convenient time to talk?"

5. In my weekly schedule have I planned
    a regular time for getting up?
    a regular bedtime?
    time alone with God?
    time alone with my husband and with each child?
    time for family devotions?
    time for myself—exercise, rest, hair, clothes?
    time for church services and activities?

10
Time on the Job

> *"Whatever you do, work
> at it with all your heart,
> as working for the Lord,
> not for men."*
> —*Colossians 3:23*

My grandfather died in the influenza epidemic of 1918. My father was just a baby, and Granny was pregnant with my aunt. With no husband and two babies to support, Granny never wondered whether or not she should work. She had to. She waited tables in a local restaurant, cooked for field hands on my uncle's farm, worked at the school cafeteria, and took in boarders. She kept a large garden and canned food, made her own soap and candles. I remember walking to school with her on winter mornings, lighting our way across the frozen ground with a flashlight. I remember the steamy windows and delicious smells as she and the other ladies made hot rolls and cobbler. "Never be ashamed to do honest work," she told me.

My mother's parents owned a dry goods store. They both worked long hours to earn a living. I remember how hard it was to wait until the store closed on Saturday nights—and especially on Christmas Eve. Before we could gather around Grandmother's big dining table for a luscious meal, then move to the living room to open those tantalizing gifts, we had to be sure all the farm families had finished their last-minute shopping.

My father owned a weekly newspaper, and my mother and my sister and I all worked on it—running the clattering linotype machine and the big, creaking printing press. Often we worked late into the night to make our weekly deadline.

In our family the women have always worked. And so have the men and children. My best girlfriend's parents owned the

local hardware store. Another friend and her widowed mother ran a farm outside of town—driving tractors and raising cattle. Mothers who just kept house and children who went out with their friends after school were a rarity.

What a surprise to move to the city and discover that the role of women was a heated issue. What some women considered a "traditional value" had been a luxury we couldn't afford. It's wonderful when women have the option of staying at home to rear their children. But for the sixty-two percent of us with children under eighteen who have jobs, the question is not, Can we hold a job and still meet the needs of our families? It is, rather, How can we do it? How can we manage our time on the job efficiently so we can serve our employers, advance our careers, and still keep our families as our first priority?

Today's working mothers have to fight for maternity leave and good child care. They have to perform up to competitive standards on the job while maintaining a home and family. They do not need a load of guilt as well.

Why do we work? To support ourselves and our families, to give to the needy and help spread the gospel, to contribute to society, to develop and use our talents, to gain personal satisfaction and self-esteem.

Christians who work have an even better reason. God made us to work. He put people in the garden and gave them work to do before sin entered the world. He's given us our hands, brains, and muscles, and he wants us to use these gifts for his glory and the good of others.

Christians should be the best workers on any job—conscientious, honest, thorough, and cheerful, quick to help and slow to take offense. As Paul told the slaves in Colossae, "not only when their eye is on you and to win their favor, but with sincerity of heart and reverence for the Lord. Whatever you do, work at it with all your heart, as working for the Lord, not for men, since you know that you will receive an inheritance from the Lord as a reward. It is the Lord Christ you are serving" (Col. 3:22–24).

Don't leave the Lord out of your work life. Strive for a union of professional and spiritual lives. See your work as an opportunity to minister. Let Jesus define success for you. Pray about your work. Pray during your commute. God will give you the strength for your day and will bless your efforts for him.

Find something to enjoy about your work. A feeling of compulsion makes work a burden. Take pride in work well done. Cultivate friends among the people you work with. Learn to care. Be thankful that you're able to work. Many people never appreciate their jobs until they retire.

A Changing Picture

In the early days when our society was pre-industrial, most people farmed, and time was measured by the seasons and the sun. With the Industrial Revolution, machines and factories dominated the work scene, and the clock not only measured time but ordered our lives as well.

Now most experts agree that our nation is in a post-industrial period. We have shifted from working with things to working with people, as service jobs draw more and more of us into offices, classrooms, and research labs. There our time is less structured, more self-directed.

Increased freedom calls for judgment in establishing priorities. All jobs involve a certain amount of routine. Even artists spend time cleaning brushes. We must accept the fact that about

My Time-Wasters on the Job—What Are They?

1. Lack of planning   Yes _____ No _____

2. Procrastination   Yes _____ No _____

3. Disorganization, messy work area   Yes _____ No _____

4. Lack of clear goals and priorities   Yes _____ No _____

5. Excuse-making and shifting blame   Yes _____ No _____

6. Overloaded schedule   Yes _____ No _____

7. Indecision   Yes _____ No _____

8. Failure to delegate   Yes _____ No _____

three-fourths of our time will be spent doing what an unskilled laborer could do.

As Christians we need to be aware of the challenges and risks posed by more flexible schedules. We must exercise self-discipline to avoid taking unfair advantage. Accepting a paycheck obligates us, not just to put in a day's work, but to do it the best we can.

Stealing Time

According to Robert Half, president of an employment firm, theft of time is the biggest crime in America. Arriving late, leaving early, taking unnecessary sick leave, socializing during work hours, being inattentive, operating a second business on the side, eating at the desk and then taking an hour off for lunch, making excessive personal phone calls, and taking long and frequent coffee breaks cost the American economy as much as $70 billion a year.

Even under the best conditions, six hours of productive work a day is about as much as any employee puts in. Still, most of us waste additional hours every day, even when we're supposedly working. There's a big difference between being busy and being effective.

At the other extreme, some companies have started cracking down on workaholics. "There's a major difference between the workaholic and the work enthusiast," says Dr. Beverly Potter, management psychologist at Stanford University. The work enthusiast has healthy motives, is striving toward a goal, and essentially enjoys her job. The workaholic, on the other hand, works to avoid loneliness or failure, doesn't enjoy the time she's at work, and is uncomfortable with unstructured time.

Christians may become workaholics out of a sense of duty, seeking to earn God's favor. "Surely I'll get caught up," we think, but we never can do enough. Accepting God's grace that we're loved and forgiven allows us to work out of gratitude, not duty.

Workaholism is an addiction rooted in inadequacy and insecurity, according to Dr. Samantha Ross, manager of patient care for a dependency treatment hospital. "You have to treat the workaholic like a gambler or an overeater." June Baldino of the American Management Association says that "female managers can be as single-minded as males, or possibly even more so."

Corporations don't want managers who set an unrealistic pace. Eugene Croisant, executive vice president of human resources for Continental Bank of Chicago, speaks of "new value workers" who work hard eight hours a day and then want a "life outside the work environment." This trend is good news for women, who generally have a full life at home on top of their jobs.

Calm, confident people—who work hard when they're on the job and know how to take off when the workday is over— inspire confidence. And one way to be calm and confident on the job is to plan and use your time wisely.

There are essentially three kinds of work—routine, productive, and creative. Routine tasks should be done in minimum time with maximum efficiency and minimum emotional effort. The more efficient you become at these tasks, the more automatic they become and the more time and energy you have for more creative work. Make habits work for you. Drill for skill.

Productive work is more satisfying. Do it and it stays done for a while. While this kind of work demands more concentration and emotional energy than purely routine tasks, it rewards us with a greater sense of accomplishment.

Creative work is the most satisfying—and most rare—of all. It brings heart, mind, and imagination into play. It allows for self-expression, stamping the job as distinctively yours. Creativity can be brought to bear on almost any job, even one which is generally considered routine or productive.

Preparation

There is no substitute for good preparation. In our age of instant gratification, we resent taking the time to learn, but preparation pays big dividends in the long run. Just as the woodcutter carefully sharpens his ax before he starts chopping trees, we need to learn all we can about the work we want to do, either through academic training or experience.

Education plays a vastly different role in job preparation today than it did twenty years ago. Some thirty percent of the work force holds college degrees, but only half of all current jobs require even a high school diploma. Some jobs require an apprenticeship or starting out at the periphery and working in as experience is gained.

Other jobs demand greater literacy skills or are becoming more technical, requiring analysis and conclusions. To meet the demand, a number of major corporations are offering basic skills courses on site.

In addition to general education, you need to learn what is expected of you in your particular job. Request a written or verbal job description, and ask about anything you don't understand. It's worth the time to get it straight.

There is no shame in learning from others. James A. Michener recalls "a sequence of notable paintings in which Titian copied, in his own good style, the work of Giovanni Bellini; and Rubens copied Titian, after making his personal adjustments; and Eugene Delacroix, a most individualistic painter, copied Rubens to probe his secrets; and Vincent van Gogh copied Delacroix." This copying was not for the purpose of imitation, but to learn.

Learning never stops. Many people today prepare for second, and even third, careers. Others prepare for advancement, and all must keep abreast of developments, study related fields, and stay alert to new opportunities.

Organization

While working mothers average only about two hours less a week on the job than their male counterparts and commute about an hour less, they are responsible for most of the housework and child-rearing when they get home as well. The woman who works at home full time spends 52–53 hours per week accomplishing her household duties, while a career woman averages at least 28 over and above her job requirements.

Working mothers can't afford to waste time on the job. They need to complete their work and go home, without overtime or a bulging briefcase. If you have a problem with time use on the job, ask yourself the following questions:

Do I take the time to plan?

Do I spend so much time on routine chores that I don't have enough left over for important jobs?

Is my desk so cluttered I have trouble finding things?

Do I spend too much time on the phone, with drop-in visitors, and in meetings?

Following these steps to organization will result in time saved in the long run:

1. Visualize

What kind of person do you want to become? What do you want to achieve? Professionally? Educationally? Personally? List specific goals and work toward them each day.

2. Plan ahead

As a member of a college publicity department, I was required to attend a staff meeting every two weeks. At the meeting, we would review what we had done the past two weeks and discuss our plans for the coming two weeks. I resented it. As the only publicity person in an office of fund-raisers, I had little interest in their lists of calls on prospective donors, and they must have been bored with my news releases. Besides, preparing

My Daily Time Log for My Job

For the woman who works outside her home a time log can be very valuable. You may feel you do not have enough time, but it will help to know where your time is actually going. Use this Time Log for one week. Remember, there is no "typical week." Don't wait until the end of the day to fill it in.

Date _____

Time	Activity	Priority (A, B, C)	Results and Plans for Improvement
8:00			
8:30			
9:00			
9:30			
10:00			
10:30			
11:00			
11:30			
12:00			
1:30			
2:00			
2:30			
3:00			
3:30			
4:00			
4:30			

As I review my log, what two or three changes would improve my effectiveness?

for the meeting took half the afternoon, and the meeting itself, the other half. I lost a full afternoon's work every other week.

Since then, however, I've come to realize that those bi-weekly pauses to review accomplishments and map out the work ahead allowed me to be much more effective the rest of the time.

A tickler file—an accordion folder with compartments marked 1–31 for each day of the month or a simpler system in your organizer—can perform much the same function. Notes about upcoming jobs can be filed early enough in the month for completion before deadline.

Check the next day's file each night, and add the jobs to your list of things to do for the day. Each morning when you arrive at work, take a few minutes to plan your day and get your paperwork in order. Many Christians use this time to approach God in prayer for direction and guidance. Combine your planning calendar and to-do list to form a daily schedule. Add appointments, both personal and professional.

3. Set priorities

Differentiate among the urgent, important, and avoidable tasks. One writer suggests prioritizing under the following categories: "Have to," "Should do," and "Want to." Do the required tasks first, then the useful, and finally those things you'd like to get done. The third category is the place your long-term goals—and those jobs with no deadline which continue to haunt you—often end up. You'll want to make some progress on these.

4. Consolidate time

About three-quarters of your day is fixed time, with specific tasks to accomplish. But it is the remaining quarter, with tasks scattered throughout the day, that determines your success or failure. Try to arrange these random moments into more usable chunks of time, or arrange some part of your work so you can pick it up in the lulls between scheduled time.

5. Allow time

Estimate the time each task will take, allowing for emergencies. Everyone has them. They are the true test of our management skills, flexibility, and resilience. Remember to build in a ten-minute cushion.

Allow time for catch up, and schedule a quiet hour. A quiet

hour is a period of peak energy, without interruption, set aside for the most difficult and demanding jobs. Discipline yourself to protect it, and then concentrate on the task at hand.

The 80/20 Principle

The 80/20 principle, first described by Vilfredo Pareto, an Italian economist, states that approximately 20 percent of what you do yields 80 percent of the results. Applying this principle to your work:

1. Which of the tasks you have to perform are the 20 percent that will bring 80 percent return?

2. Which are the 20 percent of your customers who will provide 80 percent of your sales? Are you allocating sufficient time to them?

3. Which are the 20 percent of your employees who are doing 80 percent of the work in your organization? Are you motivating them and recognizing them?

4. If you are in management, do 20 percent of your employees give you 80 percent of your problems?

5. Do 80 percent of the complaints come from 20 percent of your customers?

6. Which of the items on your to-do list make up the 20 percent that provide 80 percent of your results? Do you concentrate on them and finish them before moving on to other items?

7. Are you choosing the 20 percent of the phone calls you need to make that will provide 80 percent of their value?

6. Use peak time

Build your schedule around your energy peaks and valleys. As we have mentioned before, use your peak times for more demanding tasks, your energy lows for routine.

7. Waste time

Occasionally waste time on purpose. Don't feel guilty about watching the clouds go by or watching steam rise from a coffee cup. A brief break can be restorative.

Beware of becoming overorganized. The person who spends too much time making lists and planning schedules may be putting off doing her job. Make orderliness work for you.

8. Don't leave God at home

God can be a part of your workday without taking time you owe your employer. Reading a few verses of Scripture and praying a brief prayer can be more refreshing than a cup of coffee at break time. Some executives meet for Bible study over a brown bag lunch.

Your Work Area

Examine your work area with the eyes of an efficiency expert. Is there anything that is constantly out of reach, or are frequently used items nearby and handy? Are materials for each task grouped together? Do you have the right tools for the job? JoAnn Thomas defines an organized person as "one who is too lazy to look for things."

Arrange things close around you—your telephone, your organizer, and your current projects. The resources you need for your job should be in easy reach on a bookcase or credenza beside or behind you. If you take work home or on the road, have your briefcase open and in reach to drop things into.

Work Habits

As you organize, beware of undercutting yourself by taking on new tasks. You may say yes when you don't have time to do a good job. As one woman said, "Don't ask me. I'm too willing!"

If you're tempted to accept another job, say, "I'll check my schedule and get back to you." Ask yourself if the job relates to your goals and purposes, advances your position, or contributes to the aims of the company. Could someone else do it? Does it need to be done at all?

Trying to tackle two jobs at once generally causes us to botch both. People who deal with the public point out the advantages of concentrating on just one person at a time, no matter how long the line.

Complete what you start if it's a small job. Divide the task or set time limits for working on a larger job spread over days or weeks. If a job is so large it seems overwhelming, use what Alan Lakein calls the "Swiss cheese" method—making small holes in it. Five minutes spent on some specific aspect of the task will give you a start, and several brief sessions can get you deeply involved in the project.

Study each individual job. Is there a way to do it more efficiently? Some companies give generous incentives for time-saving suggestions, but whether your company does or not, there are the intrinsic rewards of satisfaction and time saved. Don't be a slave to your system; make your system work for you.

In the *New York World-Telegram*, Howard Whitman writes, "Plan efficient routines, but don't be rigid. When you're going well, forget the systems. Let inspiration take over. You can straighten up those papers later."

When you go home at night, leave things in good shape to start the next day. Straighten your desk. List what you need to do the next day. Number the items in order of importance. These three steps will give you a head start on your next day's work.

Working with Others

Respect the time of others. It is egotistical and rude to be late. It is also dishonest. Appointments are contracts and imply an obligation. True courtesy treats all people alike. There should be no double standard for rich and poor, employers and employees.

An open-door policy is a poor policy. If you are in a managerial position, let it be understood that there will be periods of time when your door will be shut to get some work done. Then schedule blocks of time when you're available. Set appointments. At these times put your work aside and concentrate on your visitor. Have your secretary buzz you after twenty minutes with any given person.

Train your secretary to handle correspondence, calls, appointments, and meetings. He can deal with routine mail and calls, draft replies for important correspondence, review reports and highlight items to note, arrange travel and meetings, help plan and organize. Get together first thing in the morning to plan the day.

Learn to delegate. Delegate with discretion, defining the

task carefully. Give subordinates a chance to ask questions and report potential problems. Follow up, but don't breathe down their necks. Trust your workers, and cut them some slack. Keep a record of the jobs you've delegated, and insist on deadlines.

Train a subordinate to do a job you usually do. List all your activities and divide them into critical, important, desirable, and unnecessary. Eliminate the unnecessary, delegate the desirable and some of the important to free time for the critical. Don't do anything someone else can do as well if you have the option.

Save time by putting out fires before they spread. Deal immediately with disgruntled employees, personal problems, and unmanageable work loads.

Use meetings to deal with mutual problems, not individual ones. Don't schedule a meeting if a call or memo will do. Schedule meetings late in the day to keep from wasting your prime time and that of others. Start promptly, allow time for each agenda item, and keep on track. Seek consensus, not unanimity.

Paperwork

We're all drowning in a sea of paperwork, much of which is not essential. Here are some suggestions for dealing with paperwork:

1. Read selectively, scan, ask questions about what you're reading, take notes, dictate memos as you read to pass on to others or remind yourself of future action.
2. Take some appropriate action—toss, delegate, do, or file. Don't just read something and set it aside to handle later, or you'll have to read it again. Throw out as much paperwork as possible. One busy man uses a dictating machine and handles ninety percent of his correspondence when he first picks it up.
3. Don't handle the same piece of paper twice. Every time you pick up a document, do something to advance the project. Put a check in the corner each time you handle it. Watch for too many checks.
4. If your desk is already a disaster area, begin by elimi-

nating the backlog. Clear your desk, dividing the things on it into magazines, junk mail, routine, and priority.

Go through the priority file first. Spend a couple of hours a day on it, and try to bring it up to date in three days. Then move on to the routine. If you don't have what you need for a job, put it in your follow-up or tickler file, and check it before you tackle your priority file each day. Skim magazines; photocopy articles to read later.

Once you've caught up, streamline the flow. Keep on top of paperwork. Keep your desk clear. Don't let things pile up. Move them along. Never let anything sit on your desk for more than a day.

5. File and cull files regularly. Don't let filing pile up. Jenny, a personnel officer for a large corporation, files everything immediately, dropping it into the folder and waiting to secure it until she opens the folder again. Of course, in her job it's vital not to leave papers lying around.
6. Don't copy or file things you don't need. Keep files current. Don't buy a new file cabinet.
7. Limit journals and other publications to the most helpful, and don't let them pile up. Skim, rip out or

copy, and file. Save reading for low energy periods and waits. Don't read passively. Search for ideas. Highlight. Make notes in the margins. Copy significant pages in books, highlight, and make notes. Read with a purpose.

8. If someone sorts your mail, have her divide it into two stacks: must see and discard. Some people prefer a more complex system: urgent, read and save, read and discard, file, and discard.

Phone Calls

These suggestions can help you save time on the phone:

1. Set aside a specific time each day for phone calls. Plan important calls, jotting down points to cover. Leave a message, not just your number, if that will do the job. Return calls promptly. Group call-backs.
2. Communicate clearly. Listen attentively. Make notes on calls. Have something to work on if you're put on hold.
3. If possible, have your calls screened. Prepare a list of the people you'll always talk to.
4. Friendly conversation is polite, but should be limited. Get to the point. Shirley Belz of the National Home Study Council contends that people who stay on the phone half an hour or longer are probably using you as a therapist—and you're cheating your employer if you let them. Interject some of your own problems and see how soon they'll get off the line. Silence is also effective in getting people to stop rambling after their business is finished.

Travel

Travel consumes a lot of time for many businesspeople. These suggestions will help you make better use of travel time:

1. If you fly on business, use a travel agent. Tell the agent what you're looking for—convenience or thrift—and let her take over from there.
2. Reserve your rooms in advance. Make a checklist of the

things you need to take with you. Conserve luggage space.

3. If you travel often, keep a kit packed with a small tube of toothpaste, a toothbrush, shampoo, brush, comb, and other essentials.

4. If you drive, plan a circular route with the last calls close to home.

5. Dictate on the road. Pull off and take a quiet hour. Have your briefcase equipped with what you need to schedule the next day's work, summarize reports, and update your log. Keep maps, stationery and stamps, scratch pad, calculator, pens, business cards, checks, highlighter, stapler and staples, pins, needles and thread, address book, spare keys and change for pay phones and parking meters.

The time you spend on your job is important. It represents roughly a quarter of your week. You owe it to yourself, your employer, and your God to make good use of your time on the job.

Consider the words of Helen Temple in her poem, "The Tyranny of the Trivia":

> From the tyranny
>   of the trifling,
> O Lord,
>   Deliver me.
>
> Let me not bog down
>   In the nitty-gritty,
> Spending my days
>   Shuffling memoranda
> And counting paper clips
>   While the world dies.
>
> Deliver me
>   From days spent
> Tying shoestrings,
>   Filing useless paper notes,
> Compiling endless data,
>   On inconsequential subjects,

Sitting
    In interminable sessions
Rehashing the reasons
    For not accomplishing anything.

Once in a while, Lord,
    Send a good fire,
A clean-burning, sizzling flame
    To burn out
The accumulated trivia
    Of my life.

And a sharp, piercing wind
    To whistle through
The enduring foundation
    That remains
And sweep out the ashes of the useless.
    Leaving my life
Bone bare,
    Shining clean,
And at your service.

Give me the kind of vision
    That sees through the trivia
To the essential:
    Your will
In the midst
    Of the welter
Of the insignificant.
    And having seen that,
Give me the courage
    To throw the rest away.

In the days that are left to me,
    O Lord,
Deliver me
    From the tyranny
Of the trivia,
    That I not come,
Worn-out and empty-handed,
    To meet You on that day.

Questions and Activities

1. Think of a two-career woman whom you admire. Ask her to share with you some of her priorities, problems, plans.

2. In checking your to-do list you find you have procrastinated in doing some A's. List three specific steps to stop this unproductive habit.

3. As a Christian you are a steward of your time on the job. Are you conscientiously serving your employer or company in terms of

> arrival time?
>
> quitting time?
>
> coffee breaks?
>
> lunch time?
>
> telephoning?
>
> socializing?

4. Many of us think we work best under pressure. Do we really, or do we just have to work faster because we create our own crises by delay? The next time you feel yourself rushing through a job, stop and take a deep breath and see if you can't do a better job by thinking more clearly about what you're doing.

5. The book, *The One-Minute Manager*, by Kenneth Blanchard and Spencer Johnson stresses

> A. brief, exact, written goals
>
> B. brief and specific commendation of coworkers
>
> C. brief and specific reprimands of employees concluded with encouragement

What is one specific way I can use each of these suggestions to improve my job performance?

11
Giving Myself Away

*"For we are God's
workmanship, created in
Christ Jesus to do
good works."
—Ephesians 2:10*

When we first came to Pepperdine, Norvel and I planned to start a new women's support group to augment school funds. We hadn't been here a year when I got six other women to join me in forming a steering committee to launch the Associated Women for Pepperdine. We were amazed when three hundred women showed up for an organizational brunch in our garden.

Soon we had two thousand members. Throughout its existence, the group has encouraged service beyond self. In joining hands, these women have accomplished far more than they dreamed. They have used their individual talents in a collective way to furnish scholarship funds for hundreds of students each year.

Some of these women have the gift of leadership. Others have the gifts of encouragement, promotion, and hospitality. Many have gifts of artistry—painting pictures, candlemaking, baking cakes, making candy or Christmas decorations, jewelry, clothes, hand-crocheted rugs, quilts, or fine embroidery. Each has the gift of compassionate service.

The motto of the college is "Freely ye have received, freely give." These women have received rewards in terms of fellowship, love, and the joy of contributing to the leadership of tomorrow. So often I've heard them say, "I've received so much more than I've given."

Any act of service must be focused on a purpose. God has a purpose for us. Like an inventor who sees a need and isn't content with just "wishful thinking," God set to work to fulfill his purpose.

Sometimes inventions don't do what their inventors have in mind, but inventors are persistent people. Thomas Edison, for example, tried over six thousand materials before he found the proper filament for his light bulb. Some materials created a remarkable flash. Others disintegrated. But Edison was searching for a material which would glow steadily for a long period of time. He had a purpose in mind, and he kept working till he got it right.

Unlike Edison, God didn't have to experiment. He started with nothing and created something "very good" (Gen. 1:31). He even created a procedure for re-creation, allowing us to get back on track when we've veered from his purpose.

What is this purpose? According to Paul, "We are God's workmanship, created in Christ Jesus to do good works" (Eph. 2:10). Why am I here? To do good works. How can I fulfill God's purpose? Be like Jesus, who "went around doing good" (Acts 10:38).

Jesus is the perfect example of one who gave himself for others. He made himself nothing by taking human form. He humbled himself by becoming obedient, even to death, and God exalted him. Through his example, we are challenged to "look not only to [our] own interests, but also to the interests of others" (Phil. 2:4–9).

Jesus touched his world profoundly, leaving it a far better place than it was before he came. He helped a host at a wedding, ministered to the sick, touched little children, visited the bereaved, taught one-on-one and in groups. He felt compassion and acted out of compassion, blessing those with whom he came in contact. As Henry Drummond writes, "We hear much of love to God; Christ spoke much of love to man. We make a great deal of peace with heaven; Christ made much of peace on earth."

How much impact do we as his followers have on the world today? How much does your local church impact your community? How much do you as an individual impact those in your life? "You are the light of the world. . . . Let your light shine before men, that they may see your good deeds and praise your Father in heaven" (Matt. 5:14, 16).

In sports, we distinguish between professional and amateur athletes, but there are no amateurs in the church of God. Those who are paid for their work are released to spend more time on it, but all of us, paid or unpaid, are ministers—servants of others and thus of God. We can each make a difference.

How do we do it? The same way Jesus did—by denying ourselves, submitting to God's will, and giving ourselves to others.

Finding Our Place

Our society places too high a premium on money. Automobiles are appraised in terms of resale value. Houses and neighborhoods are assessed, and we speak of upscale areas or low-rent districts. Even people are judged on the basis of income. "What is she worth?" we ask.

The women's movement exacerbated the problem, downgrading volunteer work by insisting that a salary represent the measure of our worth.

Despite such negative pressure, a recent Gallup survey indicates that more than half the nation's adults and teens— some eighty-nine million people—volunteer their time, either in individual or organized service projects.

According to Brian O'Connell, president of Independent Sector, the group which commissioned the study, "We have found this is still very much a caring country."

"We are particularly astounded," O'Connell adds, "to find that the woman who works is more likely to contribute her time than the homemaker. This absolutely explodes the myth of the decline in volunteerism because of the working woman."

Exposure may be one reason working women volunteer. As my friend Dale said, "I didn't realize how serious a problem homelessness was until I started my new job downtown and saw it for myself. Now I want to do something about it."

Those who volunteer their time are also more likely to contribute money to charities. Half of the contributors come from families whose income is less than $20,000 a year. "This is the only country in the world where giving and volunteering are

characteristic of the entire nation, across all economic groups,"
O'Connell says.

"But I don't have time," you may say. "After I work all day
and get a few things done at home, the day is over." Or, "Here I
am with two babies at home, and you want me to do volunteer
work?" Or, "I have a job and am going to school. I don't have
time for service projects."

While there are many worthwhile projects that need and
deserve our support, we need to wake up to the opportunities for
service right where we are. Jesus helped the people he encountered in his daily life. Are we modeling ourselves after him if we
ignore people at work, criticize salespeople in the store, nag our
families at home, and then hurry off to knock on doors or pass
out magazines in a hospital?

If we work outside the home or go to school, let's learn to
forget ourselves and concentrate on those around us, looking for
opportunities to serve and encourage. If we have children, we
should first live and teach Christ at home. Our home, in turn,
influences the broader world as we invite guests in, get to know
our neighbors and our children's friends, and become involved
in our schools and communities.

Thus, our worship assemblies take on a new role. Rather
than serving God a few hours a week through worship, we serve
him full time, stopping to commune with him and with each
other and to be fed on his Word to gain strength for further
service.

Areas of Service

Even though we all have periods in our lives when we are
unable to give time to organized projects, there are other times
when we are free to do so. Many groups and efforts deserve our
support, and while we should avoid saying yes to more than we
can handle, we should be careful not to say no all the time. As
someone has said, "If not by me, by whom? If not now, when?"

Among the places we can volunteer our time are the
following:

1. Church

With more women working and more options for discretionary time, our churches are experiencing a shortage of workers. There is always a need for teachers—for children's classes, ladies' classes, prospects, and new converts.

Young people need chaperones who are willing to drive, host, and help out with youth projects. Elsie, a public schoolteacher, spent one Saturday washing cars with the young people to raise money for their trip to Magic Mountain and most of the next Saturday driving them there and staying to chaperone.

There is always a need for visits—to the sick and bereaved, to new members and visitors, and those who are in danger of falling away. Lela and her chicken soup are famous among one group of Christian shut-ins.

Some have the talent to help with the church's finances or write for church publications. Others can do gardening or painting or clean-up. Volunteer for at least one of the organized programs of service at church.

2. Schools

Our public and private schools are suffering from spiraling costs and cutbacks in funding—and our children suffer as a result. Volunteers are needed in the classroom, in PTA and other fund-raising programs, on the principal's council and other advisory groups, and in support organizations for Christian colleges and universities. I've worked in each of these capacities over the years.

Foster Grandparents is a special program which benefits both the young and the retirees who participate, as well as freeing teachers to concentrate on teaching. For years, Evelyn, a grandmotherly sort of person, has served as a member of the board of trustees for a Christian college. Not only that, but she has purchased fabric and made clothing to sell to raise money for scholarships.

3. Charities

The shortage of funds has created a demand for volunteers to raise funds for hospitals and special schools and to give time working directly with the elderly, the ill, and the handicapped. Upon her retirement, Gladys began working a few mornings a week as a volunteer aid at a school for the junior blind, helping students on an individual basis and chaperoning class outings. The children benefit from her efforts, and Gladys has a satisfying outlet for her energies.

Hunger, both at home and abroad, is a growing problem. Marilyn is a department chairperson at a major state university, but one day a week she spends her lunch hour serving at a soup kitchen. Louise volunteers with Para Los Ninos, a shelter for homeless children.

Those who have experienced a problem should be particularly eager to reach out to others. Marla suffered from Epstein-Barr virus, and as she began to recover, she started counseling other women with the disease. Christine had cancer. Now she visits and encourages cancer patients in the hospital.

4. Social welfare

There is a growing need for workers in youth programs, drug abuse prevention, gang intervention, and prison visitation. Fred and Willa adopted a reform school inmate, writing and visiting her regularly, then helped her get a job and adjust to life when she was released.

Problems in our schools, together with the influx of people from other countries, are creating a need for literacy training, programs teaching English as a second language, and other efforts to help newcomers. During the amnesty program, Roberto donated hours of his time to filling out application forms, a service lawyers charged $500 to $1,500 to perform. Betty took a Japanese student into her home and helped him get an apartment and a car.

5. Community service

Our society has become so complex that we can no longer depend on Washington or the schools or even our churches to meet local needs. Politics shouldn't be a dirty word to Christians. In our representative democracy, we are the government, and we must do our part to improve the quality of life for all our citizens.

At the grass-roots level, we can promote a recycling program—to clean up a river, plant trees or flowers. Margie wrote letters to government officials and mobilized her neighbors to stop construction of a hazardous waste dump in her neighborhood. Dale works to elect candidates for public office and canvasses on foot and by phone on behalf of conservation projects.

6. Individual efforts

Those who prefer not to work in organized programs shouldn't feel left out. Adopt a shut-in to call, write, and visit. Find a child who needs tutoring. Gather clothing and other items you are using no longer and, rather than have a garage sale, give them to the church or the Salvation Army.

Louise takes food, clothing, and blankets downtown to hand

Discovering My Spiritual Gifts

To rethink my efforts as a volunteer, I will seek to rediscover my gifts by studying the lists of gifts of the Holy Spirit given to "prepare God's people for works of service" (Eph. 4:12).

Romans 12:8–10
   Serving
   Teaching
   Encouraging
   Contributing
   Leading
   Showing Mercy

1 Corinthians 12:27–28
   Teaching
   Helping
   Administering

Ephesians 4:11–12
   Preparing others for service
   Building up the body

1 Peter 4:10–11
   "Each one should use whatever gift he has received to serve others, faithfully administering God's grace in its various forms."

out among the homeless. The women in our Bible class distribute sandwiches and juice there once a month.

There is much to be done and never enough people to do it. How can we best serve?

1. Assess your gifts. Our service takes as many forms as our abilities. "Having gifts that differ according to the grace given to us, let us use them," Paul says (Rom. 12:6 RSV). And Peter explains, "Each one should use whatever gift he has received to serve others" (1 Peter 4:10).

2. Study the needs. Be informed. Consider the needs of church, schools, charities, communities, and individuals.

3. Choose what you can handle. Consider your own circumstances, interests, resources and abilities. What can you do to help? One handicapped woman in her

mid-thirties led 521 people to Christ in four years through World Bible School correspondence work. At one point, she had three thousand students in seven African nations.

4. Accept training. Don't assume you know everything about an effort. Hone your skills. Be open to growth.

5. Learn to involve others. Janis Schlack tells of a friend who asked her for donations of money, clothing, toys, food, or medical supplies for orphanages in South America. Janis was "too busy, tired, and poor" to do much about it, but she wrote letters to two schools, two ministers, and two newspapers, explaining the program and asking their support. "The response was almost unbelievable!" she says. "I collected $1,000 and 1,500 pounds of supplies."

6. Be a servant leader. Of his wife Rosalynn's efforts to help provide low-cost housing for the poor, former president Jimmy Carter writes, "She has never been more beautiful than when her face was covered with black smut from scraping burned ceiling joists, and streaked with sweat from carrying sheets of plywood from the street level up to the floor where we were working, cutting subflooring with a power saw, and nailing it down with just a few hard hammer blows."

7. Be positive. Find joy in your efforts. Hold them up to God in prayer, and trust him to bring good from them. "Therefore, my dear brothers, stand firm. Let nothing move you. Always give yourselves fully to the work of the Lord, because you know that your labor in the Lord is not in vain" (1 Cor. 15:58).

8. Be persistent. The little I can do may seem insignificant, and maybe it is—by itself. But all of us together can accomplish great things. As Whoopi Goldberg reminds us, if each of us gave five hours a week to our favorite cause, we would be the equivalent of twenty million full-time volunteers.

As Christians, we should be like a hone, which wears itself out making many blades sharp. Will we wear out or rust out?

9. Learn to say no. Once you have chosen your areas of service, learn to say no to other requests that come your way. Give a straightforward explanation of what you're unwilling to do, and propose an alternative. Clarify the reasons you are not willing to participate. Express your interest and moral support, but hold firmly to your decision, knowing that you are being true to the call God has made on your time.

Failure to say no can cause you to be taken for granted. It can trap you in situations you can't handle. It can cause you to lose sight of your own priorities. It can encourage others to neglect their responsibilities. At the very least, it will cause you to be overextended.

It's Good for You

Although our own welfare is not the primary motivation for serving others, volunteerism is good for us. A decade-long study of 2,700 people by the University of Michigan found that doing volunteer work increases life expectancy. Volunteering can strengthen the heart and the immune system.

People need people, and a connection with people is more

healthful than isolation. According to pioneer stress researcher Hans Selye, the warmth of altruism decreases stress, while anger and hostility increase the risk of illness.

The scale of life today—the overwhelming size of our cities and institutions—removes the personal touch and creates distrust. A warm, caring individual who is seeking to help can mean a lot to those who are frustrated by red tape and bureaucratic runarounds.

Volunteer work helps confirm our common humanity. As George Washington Carver said, "How far you go in life depends on your being tender with the young, compassionate with the aged, sympathetic with the striving and tolerant of the weak and strong. Because someday in your life you will have been all of these."

Altruism blocks depression, helps us overcome feelings of inadequacy, and gives meaning to life. Only that person who has learned to fill her time with efforts for others and for some cause beyond herself is free from the emptiness which can result when we use our time only for self or trivialities. It does "take time to be holy." Many people don't want to be holy, but all of us want serenity, courage, and faith, and these resources come only from prayer, worship, and selfless service.

Remember the poor widow who saved herself and her child by sharing the last of her food with the prophet Elijah. As Elizabeth Charles has written,

> Is thy cruse of comfort failing? Rise and share it with
> another,
>> And through all the years of famine it shall serve thee
>> and thy brother.
> Love divine will fill the storehouse, or thy handful still
> renew;
>> Scanty fare for one will often make a royal feast for
>> two.
> For the heart grows rich in giving; all its wealth is living
> grain;
>> Seeds which mildew in the garner, scattered, fill with
>> gold the plain.
> Is thy burden hard and heavy? Do thy steps drag wearily?

Help to bear thy brother's burden; God will bear both
it and thee.

Questions and Activities

1. Because I want to reach out beyond myself and my family, I
will memorize these lines and find ways to implement their
resolve:
But I am only one
I cannot do everything
But I can do something
Because I cannot do everything
I will not refuse to do
The something I can do.

2. As a parent I will seek to encourage the potential of my
children by giving them opportunities, training, and inspiration
for service outside our home by

A. setting an example of service to others in my church and
community.

B. getting to know my children's special interests and
abilities.

C. introducing my children to adults who are giving
themselves in Christian service.

D. building their sense of confidence and self-worth by
providing opportunities which do not overwhelm them
but challenge them to give themselves in service.

E. letting them see the joy and satisfaction I receive by
loving service outside our home.

3. God wants more than involvement of our hands. He wants
commitment of our hearts. To be sure that our service is
motivated by love and sacrifice and sharing, I will pray once a
day every day this week for God to make me more like his
greatest servant, his Son.

4. To help me discover my gifts I will remember:

A. They are gifts. I don't deserve them nor do I create
them. They are to be used to his glory.

B. One gift is not greater than another. I will not overestimate the importance of my gifts. Neither will I underestimate their importance. There is no room for arrogance or envy. No competition. No inferiority.

C. I will pray that God will guide me to know my particular gift or gifts.

D. I will explore possibilities. I will get involved.

E. I will examine my own feelings. Usually a person likes to do what she is gifted to do.

F. What do my spiritually minded friends think are my gifts?

G. I will be sure that my gifts are used to serve others, to build up the church.

5. An analysis of spiritual gifts such as "Trenton Spiritual Gifts Analysis" may help you see how you are equipped to serve. It can be ordered from Charles E. Fuller Institute of Evangelism and Church Growth, P. O. Box 901990, Pasadena, CA 91009-1990.

12
The Seasons
of My Life

> *"When I became a [woman], I put childish ways behind me."*
> *—1 Corinthians 13:11*

It's been half a month now. It's better—like half a month after a funeral—but the weird thing is that I still don't know what died." That's what I wrote in my journal that bleak September day, a week after my fortieth birthday. I was married to a wonderful man. We had two bright, attractive children. I had a satisfying career with a religious publishing company, was teaching a Bible class and speaking for women's groups, and was engaged in my lifetime dream of writing books. I should have felt fulfilled and satisfied, but I'd just spent most of two weeks in tears.

It's called midlife crisis—that point somewhere between thirty-five and forty-five when you realize that your marriage, your children, your career, your house—even yourself— haven't lived up to your expectations. And they aren't likely to get much better. You aren't one of the "fine young couples" at church anymore. You aren't young anymore. You've reached the top of whatever hill you've been climbing, and it's all downhill from there.

Of course, turning forty wasn't as bad as it seemed at the time. But it made me realize that, just as I'd studied the developmental stages of children and teens, I needed to give thought to my own development.

According to UCLA psychologist Roger Gould, "A person does not possess the full range of his uniqueness after merely passing through adolescence, which is the last stage of mental development that many psychologists officially recognize."

Life is change. We change. "While children mark the passing years by changing their bodies," Gould says, "adults change with their minds. Passing years and events slowly accumulate, like a viscous wave, eventually releasing their energy and assuming new forms in altered relationships with both time and people."

In the Genesis account of the Flood, after the waters had abated and the earth was dry, Noah built an altar and worshiped God. And God promised never again to destroy all life from the earth. "As long as the earth endures," he told Noah, "seedtime and harvest, cold and heat, summer and winter, day and night will never cease" (Gen. 8:22). God promised an orderly progression of the seasons of the natural world, and of life on it, as long as the earth remained.

In general terms, we experience similar seasons in our lives. Although a young person can be surprisingly mature or an older person, young at heart, we all pass through a springtime of youth and growth, a summer of nurturing and productivity, an autumn of the maturing of our fruits, and a winter of calm completion and eventual death.

Our stage of life has a great deal to do with the way we manage our time. Our priorities, responsibilities, and energy vary with the changing seasons. But most importantly, we need to see our lives, not just in terms of today or this week or even the next five years. We need to manage our time with the perspective of our lives as a whole.

God established our personal timetable as surely as he did the seasons of the world around us. To live fully in each of these seasons of life, we need to be aware of both the challenges and the threats they pose.

Spring

"These are the best years of your life. Don't waste them," an older woman told a high school junior. The girl wrinkled her face. This is the best there is? she thought, thinking over her lonely Saturday nights, insecurity in new situations, and unpredictable menstrual periods and outbursts of acne.

No matter how great they look in retrospect, the late teen years are the first crisis point in adulthood. It is an age of becoming, of gaining a distinct, separate identity. "Who am I?" we ask ourselves. "What kind of person do I want to be?" We seek the answer in education, career preparation, and dating.

Spring is a time of breaking out. Buds explode from their cases, birds from their eggs. Observing the outward beauty, we may not be aware of the violence of the changes occurring inside.

Change always brings pain, and youth is a period of rapid change. Bodies expand and develop in alarming ways. Attitudes are volatile and moods may swing wildly. Who hasn't observed or experienced the teen-ager who alternates between wanting to be independent and wanting to be mothered? We don't know which stage to expect next, and she doesn't either.

In our twenties we tend toward religious legalism. We have high ideals and expect people to live up to them, with very little patience with failure on the part of ourselves or others.

Young people are moving away from their parents. Opposing this natural direction may only foster rebellion and cause it to break out with greater intensity later. Gaining independence and self-esteem helps a young person accept responsibility and resist conformity.

Youth is an age of choice. In addition to the choice of basic commitments and values, it is a time to choose directions which will influence the rest of life: Should I go to college? Which one? Should I get a job? Get married? Have children?

It is important to recognize the full extent of the options. In the church we have often been guilty of teaching that marriage is the only acceptable option for a young woman. Despite Paul's clear teaching, there has been little appreciation of the place of the single in the church or in society.

Our limited concept of choices may make it difficult for our young people to gain their independence. So can the extended period of schooling and the high cost of living. It's hard for a young, single person to be entirely self-supporting.

Kathy is a twenty-year-old college student. During the school term, she lives with three roommates in an on-campus apartment—doing her own cooking and cleaning and coming and going as she pleases. She has worked summers since she was sixteen, contributing most of the difference between the cost of her education and the scholarships, grants, and loans she receives.

CAREER?
SCHOOL?
MARRIAGE?

But every summer she moves back in with her parents. It's a difficult adjustment for all concerned. Kathy is accustomed to being on her own. Her parents, on the other hand, like to know where she's going and when to expect her home, and they want her to help out around the house. Her mother drives her to work because she doesn't have a car, although her boyfriend often picks her up. In many ways Kathy is independent, but like many young adults, she feels caught in transit.

Kathy's problems will be resolved with time. In the late twenties, the question shifts from "Who?" to "How?" as skills are learned, intimacy is developed, and a lifestyle is established. Although there are still many choices to be made, few are irrevocable. There is time to learn, grow, and experiment.

We were in our twenties when my husband came home from the military and changed his major. We decided to start a family, and I gave up my career in college publicity for a job I could do at home. But still it wasn't easy. As Gail Sheehy points out, "The woman who married early in her twenties . . . can seldom be faithful to a career in the way a man can. She is not yet practiced or confident enough in any area to integrate all her competing priorities."

Summer

If changes haven't been made earlier, choices made in the twenties may seem restrictive in the early thirties. Many who decided to remain single, to pursue careers, or not have children are having second thoughts. Others who had children early and chose to remain at home go back to work when the children start to school.

Celebrating the Seasons of a Woman's Life

Spring: "Remember your Creator in the days of your youth" (Eccl. 12:1)

Summer: "She watches over the affairs of her household and does not eat the bread of idleness. Her children arise and call her blessed; her husband also, and he praises her" (Prov. 31:27–28)

Autumn: "Charm is deceptive, and beauty is fleeting; but a woman who fears the Lord is to be praised" (Prov. 31:30)

Winter: "I was young and now I am old, yet I have never seen the righteous forsaken or their children begging bread" (Ps. 37:25).

—arranged by Judy Miller

Sarah married after receiving her master's degree. She continued pursuing her career and became director of student life at a university. After nine years, she and her husband decided to have children. It's been a difficult transition, but she chose to stay at home with them. Sarah is extremely career-oriented, and her decision has been a real sacrifice—personally and financially. But even when she takes an occasional part-time job, child-care costs are astronomical.

Eventually, however, people in their thirties settle down to growth and expansion. As Sheehy points out, by thirty or thirty-five most women have learned to handle the dual career of homemaker and "extrafamilial" worker. But these lazy days of summer appear deceptively simple on the surface. Summer is a time of teeming life and fruit-bearing. The days are so full and productive, they seem to fly by. Couples raise children and rise in their careers. Houses are built and homes are established. The focus shifts from the couple to the children.

The myriad demands can tax our resources almost to the breaking point. It is easy to stumble through our days in a haze of details and fail to appreciate them as part of an overall pattern.

There is a tendency during this period of increased demand and limited resources to put life on the back burner. "After the children are grown" or "when we get some extra money" becomes a familiar refrain. While some things may have to be postponed, life is now. We need to enjoy it for itself—despite its problems, perplexities, and demands.

How many mothers look forward to their children growing up only to find the empty nest lonely and frustrating? Children should be enjoyed while they are young, because they are soon grown and gone.

Career women need to see the broader contribution they're making rather than just the immediate chore. Learn to find enjoyment in your work. Flex the muscles of body, mind, and spirit by trying to make a success of the moment. Keep abreast, live fully, engage the present. Don't escape into mindless activity to avoid it.

Marilyn is a single woman in her thirties who has learned to cherish the present moment and fill it full of good friends and interaction. She directs a counseling center where she helps troubled people all day long. She gives herself to each one—whether an alcoholic, a pregnant teenager, parents of troubled children, a husband or wife ready to give up on marriage, or a depressed single. The counselees often get her number and call her at home at night, making it difficult for her to get away from work.

She has a lovely home in which she entertains frequently. She confides in her older sister and takes her nieces and nephews shopping. Her relationship with her Lord is strong and sustaining. But she is beginning to recognize the need for an interest outside of home and work—something she can enjoy which will take her mind off her job.

Now is the time to stretch the mold. Marilyn is wise enough to know she shouldn't wait until it is further set before she tries to break out.

I was in my thirties—feeling rather tied down with two preschoolers and a job which I was able to do at home—when I started writing a novel. At first I could only work between the hours of 11 P.M. and 2 A.M., but as the children grew, I found more time for my hobby.

Jess Lair, the author of *I Ain't Much, Baby—But I'm All I've Got*, collapsed with a heart attack at thirty-five years of age. A hard-driving businessman with a job he hated, he reviewed his life and concluded, "From now on I am never again going to do something that I don't deeply believe in."

When he recuperated, he went back to school, earned a Ph.D. in psychology, moved his family to Montana, and found a teaching job at a state university.

In a sense we *are* all we have, and we must take care of ourselves. Let things go occasionally and get some rest. Stop to smell the flowers. Take the broader view. Realize that the problems which loom so large today won't be there tomorrow.

Be aware of your place in the continuum of history. Look back at people in other times who have been where you are now.

Look ahead to life's next stage, and prepare to release today's responsibilities in order to pick up new ones. Look up from time to time and rechart your direction.

Sir Francis Chichester wanted to be the first man to fly the Atlantic alone, but Lindbergh beat him to it. So he decided to fly from New Zealand to Australia across the Tasman Sea, a more difficult route. Time after time the clouds closed in. When the sun occasionally broke through, Chichester headed for that patch of sunlight to take a new setting.

It's the same with life. We need to look up and regain our bearings. Where am I going? Is it a valid destination? Am I getting off course? Or are the things I'm doing bringing me closer to my goal?

As the summer grows to a close, we become aware of our limitations, of the limited time we have, and of our limited ability to make a real impact on the world. We may be shocked to realize how little we've accomplished. Failing to achieve the dreams of youth may lead to disillusionment and depression.

"Loss is real at this stage," David Neff writes in *Christianity Today*. "Loss of goals. Loss of energy. Loss of a sense of accomplishment. Loss of family pride. Loss of friends. And loss of faith." As we face these losses we learn to forgive ourselves and others and to appreciate God's forgiveness. And we learn a new definition of success.

Autumn

Autumn is a time of harvest, of reaping the benefits of the previous seasons. A mellow time, it can be a period of great reward as children you have touched grow into adulthood and projects you have contributed toward come to fruition.

It is a time of evaluation. As time passes increasingly faster, midlife adults examine their achievements and question whether they've been successful, fulfilled their obligations, and learned something in the process.

Values shift from activities to people, as couples are able to focus again on one another, develop deeper friendships, and serve as mentors for the young. Responsibilities shift as our children establish homes of their own and our aging parents come to depend more on us.

With the fulfillment of many of the demands of the previous periods, there is time for new activities. Just as the length of the autumn period is expanding, so are its possibilities. As Gail Sheehy points out, "Secondary interests which have been tapped earlier in life can in middle and old age blossom into a serious lifework. Each tap into a new vessel releases in the late years another reservoir of energy."

Margaret Kozeluh, a 67-year-old widow who works on the night shift at Frito-Lay, recently completed a college degree begun almost fifty years ago but interrupted while she reared her thirteen children.

"What did I get out of it?" she asks. "I majored in cultural anthropology. It is a good idea to know your fellow man, to know about other cultures. I have to say it has been lots of fun."

How could she compete with her younger classmates? "When I went to school, we were taught how to study," she says. "These young kids think they have the world by the tail, but they don't know the world from a hole in the wall. On one test they sauntered into the room, talking about the latest party. They got low scores and I got one of the highest scores."

Skills and demands have become better matched, so we exude a grace and confidence seldom found in earlier periods. Sheehy notes that the artistry of the mature is "not so white-hot, more sculpted, considered," and that the "initial product is not the finished one." The mature woman has learned to polish her work.

I learned this lesson as I found myself rewriting the novel I had started in my early thirties. When I finally got it right, I knew I'd done something to be proud of. What a publisher will think is another matter, but I did achieve, at least to my own satisfaction, what I set out to do thirteen years earlier.

The autumn years bring the potential for great service and creativity. "The direction of change is toward becoming more tolerant of oneself," Gould says, "and more appreciative of the complexity of both the surrounding world and of the mental milieu, but there are many things that can block, slow down, or divert that process." Unfortunately, the autumn of life can be an empty time if we fail to prepare for it by developing new interests or if we waste our time in fruitless yearnings for previous seasons.

Medical advances assure us of increased longevity, and smaller families give us time for greater productivity. Fifty years ago, the age of sixty-five was the winter of life. Now nearly twenty million people—nearly ten percent of the population—are over sixty-five. And they are healthier and more active than ever before. Rather than looking back in longing to earlier stages, those of us in the autumn of our lives should strive to improve the quality of these "extra years."

As Tournier says, "True happiness is always linked with deep, inner harmony. It therefore always implies acceptance of one's age: the acceptance of no longer being a child when one has reached the age of adulthood and the giving up of the goals of active life when one is advanced in years."

Winter

The fastest-growing segment of our population is made up of those over eighty—those in the winter of life. Beneath its hoary calm, winter is another time when much is happening. Death comes most often in winter, but even in the presence of death, we find the seeds of resurrection. Sad indeed is the life which is lived without an awareness of this fourth and crowning stage. What have we gained if we've only learned how to live and not how to die?

Still, there is no reason to rush it. A ninety-three-year-old man who was moving to a local nursing home took one look at a large room where people much younger than he sat staring silently into space and quipped, "Well, one thing's for sure; if I come here, we are going to have to turn this *waiting* room into a *living* room!"

His attitude was not something he'd adopted the day before. It came from a lifetime of preparation. Having lived fully the first three seasons of life, he saw no reason to stop now.

Aging may mean fewer choices, physical restrictions, and the loss of friends, but it can bring greater vision and spiritual depths. We can make younger friends. And we can reach out in

service. As Tournier says, "We have to give up all sorts of things and accept with serenity the prospect of death while remaining as active, as sociable and friendly as we can, despite an unavoidable measure of loneliness."

Ninety-one-year-old Myrtie Howell writes letters of encouragement to seventeen prison inmates from her Columbus, Georgia, nursing home. According to Charles Colson, "Myrtie has . . . corresponded with hundreds of inmates, up to forty at a time, becoming a one-woman ministry reaching into prisons all over America."

In addition to her ministry, Myrtie spends her time studying her Bible and praying. "The Lord don't need no quitters," she says. "Once in a while old Satan tells me I'm getting too old. . . . But we mustn't listen to him." Those who have benefited from her ministry are glad she hasn't.

"The real problem is not whether to do this rather than that, but what is the significance for us of what we are doing: whether it is merely in order to pass the time, or whether it is the expression of a vital need to keep on growing and developing our personality right to the end," Tournier explains.

Time is our greatest resource. Rather than waste it in fear of death, we need to embrace it and use whatever resources we have. Then, when we come to the end of our time, we can die with dignity, secure in the knowledge that we have grown steadily closer to the source of all life.

As the writer of Ecclesiastes put it,

There is a time for everything, and a season for every activity under heaven:

a time to be born and a time to die,
a time to plant and a time to uproot,
a time to kill and a time to heal,
a time to tear down and a time to build,
a time to weep and a time to laugh,
a time to mourn and a time to dance,
a time to scatter stones and a time to gather them,
a time to embrace and a time to refrain,
a time to search and a time to give up,
a time to keep and a time to throw away,
a time to tear and a time to mend,
a time to be silent and a time to speak,
a time to love and a time to hate,
a time for war and a time for peace. . . .

I know that there is nothing better for men [and women] than to be happy and do good while they live. That everyone may eat and drink, and find satisfaction in all his toil—this is the gift of God. I know that everything God does will endure forever; nothing can be added to it and nothing taken from it. God does it, so men [and women] will revere him.

—Ecclesiastes 3:1–8, 12–14

The Bible Speaks of Aging

Aging can be a blessing:

"You, however, will go to your fathers in peace and be buried at a good old age" (Gen. 15:15).

Aging is a sign of God's power:

"And if you walk in my ways and obey my statutes and commands as David your father did, I will give you a long life" (1 Kings 3:14).

"With long life will I satisfy him and show him my salvation" (Ps. 91:16).

"My son, do not forget my teaching, but keep my commands in your heart, for they will prolong your life many years and bring you prosperity" (Prov. 3:1–2).

The aged are characterized by wisdom:

"Is not wisdom found among the aged? Does not long life bring understanding?" (Job 12:12).

The aged are to be respected and cared for:

"If anyone does not provide for his relatives, and especially for his immediate family, he has denied the faith and is worse than an unbeliever" (1 Tim. 5:8).

"Honor your father and your mother" (Deut. 5:16).

"Rise in the presence of the aged, show respect for the elderly and revere your God" (Lev. 19:32).

Old age can be rich:

"They will still bear fruit in old age, they will stay fresh and green" (Ps. 92:14).

God is near the aged:

"Even to your old age and gray hairs I am he, I am he who will sustain you. I have made you and will carry you; I will sustain you and I will rescue you" (Isa. 46:4).

Questions and Activities

1. Study all the Scriptures on singles (especially 1 Corinthians 7 and the life of Paul, the apostle) and see the important place God has assigned the gift of singleness.

2. As an "older woman" (all of us are older than someone), you can be an example to the younger women and teach them as Titus 2:3–5 tells us to do. List three ways you can best fulfill this command.

3. As I contemplate the season of life I am now in, how do I resist:

    A. the narcissism, the selfishness, the me-first attitude of our generation?

    B. the cynicism created by disappointment in myself and others?

    C. the materialism and emphasis on things which characterize our age?

    D. the fear that I will be a burden to others, that I will run out of money, that I will be in pain, that I will be an invalid, that I will be forgotten or unappreciated?

4. As I contemplate the season of my life I am now in, how do I enjoy the present moment and avoid living in either the past or the future?

5. How can I develop a greater empathy for those in my season of life who need my help? How can I develop a greater empathy for those in a different season of life?

    A. What friend from the past can I reach out to today?

    B. Who is a teenager whose fears and dreams I can share?

    C. Who are some of the children in my church to whom I can show a special interest?

    D. What older person would benefit from my calls or visits?

13
Eternity
in My Heart

*"Set your minds on
things above."*
—Colossians 3:2

It wasn't until my father died a few years ago that death became
real to me. I suddenly felt exposed at the edge of the
generations. This massive figure, who had been my buffer from
danger, was gone. But it wasn't until a series of results from pap
smears raised the specter of cancer that I became fully aware of
my own mortality. I remember standing in the shower, tears
streaming down my face, as I contemplated the future of my
husband and two children without me.

It is humbling to realize that the world can continue without a
person who has been at the center of our universe. And it's even
more humbling to realize that it can go on without us.

Death is an enemy. It is the result of sin and the work of Satan
in the world. We fear it, hate it, and do everything in our power
to stall it. Yet, as Elbert Hubbard has said, "Do not take life too
seriously. You will never get out of it alive." We are dying every
moment that we live. "There is a time for everything, and a
season for every activity under heaven: a time to be born and a
time to die" (Eccl. 3:1–2).

Death is real, and the very brevity of our lives has value:

1. It gives us the opportunity to see our state clearly and
   repent. "Now is the day of salvation" (2 Cor. 6:2).
2. It motivates us to live a distinctive lifestyle. "Since
   everything will be destroyed in this way, what kind of
   people ought you to be?" (2 Peter 3:11).

3. It allows us to appreciate life with a heightened awareness of its worth. "Give glory to the Lord your God before he brings the darkness" (Jer. 13:16).
4. It impels us to service. "We must do the work of him who sent me. Night is coming, when no one can work" (John 9:4).

Release from Bondage

When my husband and I were in school in Abilene, Texas, one of our favorite places to visit was the old Guitar Mansion. Once the beautiful home of a wealthy family, it had been deserted for some time. Windows were broken, everything of value had been removed, but that massive shell of a house kept drawing us back. Maybe its very size appealed to us, living as we were in cramped student housing.

There was a way to get in through the basement, which housed a bowling alley among other refinements. But we would move quickly up the stairs to the spacious, sunny rooms above. There were fireplaces, stairways, decorative moldings of crumbling plaster. Everywhere was evidence of artistry and attention to detail. And everywhere was evidence of decay.

The Bible speaks of the "bondage of decay" enslaving the whole of creation, a bondage which will end only with "our adoption as sons, the redemption of our bodies" (Rom. 8:21–23).

Thank God, physical death is not the end of our existence. For the Christian, the end of time is a glorious release from bondage—our bondage to time. At death we put off the limitations of flesh and human nature and put on immortality (1 Cor. 15:51–53). But the process has already begun, for even though outwardly we are aging, "inwardly we are being renewed day by day. For our light and momentary troubles are achieving for us an eternal glory that far outweighs them all" (2 Cor. 4:16–17).

How do we react to this release from time with its hope and its threat? According to Paul Tillich, "Probably most of us react by looking at the immediate future, anticipating it, working for it, hoping for it, and being anxious about it, while cutting off from our awareness the future which is farther away, and above all, by cutting off from our consciousness the end, the last moment of our future." In other words, we try to avoid the thought of death.

Our whole society seems to be denying death. Older people are separated from us into retirement communities and nursing homes. Many today don't even have funerals when their loved ones die. We don't want to face decay and death.

Ruby Morrow Young took another tack. She wanted to spend Christmas with her grandchildren in our home in California. In her late seventies, she had had two strokes and lived in recognition of the possibility of a third. "But," she said, "God is as close to California as he is to Tennessee." So she made her plans.

Ruby and her husband flew to Los Angeles and enjoyed Christmas with her four grandchildren. When Norvel came home from the Orient on January 1, we all drove to Pasadena the next day to see the beautiful, flower-bedecked floats from the Rose Parade. That evening we went to prayer meeting at the Vermont Avenue Church near the campus, and afterward sat by the fireplace for a good visit.

That night Ruby suffered her fatal stroke. But she was prepared both spiritually and physically. In a special box in her closet in Nashville was a dress she had chosen to be buried in, and a letter written in her own hand containing plans for her funeral service. Bob Neil was to sing several hymns, including "In the Land of Fadeless Day" and "Beyond the Sunset." Jim Bill McInteer and Batsell Barrett Baxter were to speak. It was not at all morbid.

Ruby always planned ahead, and she was ready for this final trip. In a way, her planning freed her to get on with living. To me she lived in a beautiful balance between loving life and having the faith that death "is better by far."

With so much evasion and denial of the reality of death, I am thankful for her spiritual maturity and example.

The Eternal Now

The ancient Greeks first conceived of time as two-tiered— Being and Becoming. Being was perfect and changeless, the true reality. Becoming was imperfect and changing, the temporal world. For us as Christians, Being is eternity or God, while Becoming is time or our present lives.

The thirteenth-century German mystic Meister Eckhart said that God is outside time and that all is simultaneous to him. He spoke of the "eternal now" in the flux of time.

We must not get too busy with the things of time to think about eternal things. As Rick Atchley expressed it, "I want to talk about restoring eternity in the church. My generation is so 'now' oriented that we have almost forgotten about eternity." And Paul Tillich says, "There is no other way of judging time than to see it in light of the eternal." And, just as we need the perspective of the stages of life in managing our time, we also need the broad perspective of eternity.

For time-bound beings like ourselves, eternity is not an easy concept to grasp. It's like the two-dimensional figures of Edwin

A. Abbott's *Flatland*. As circles, squares, and triangles, they couldn't comprehend a ball breaking through the plain on which they lived. In a similar manner, eternity can be conceived of as a fifth dimension, outside of time, but still encompassing it.

Although many see eternity as beginning at death or at the end of time and continuing into the future as an extension of time, the Bible does not agree. T.S. Eliot expressed the view of many when he wrote, "To believe in the supernatural is not simply to believe that after living a successful, material, and fairly virtuous life here one will continue to exist in the best-possible substitute for this world, or that after living a starved and stunted life here one will be compensated with all the good things one has gone without." Rather, "it is to believe that the supernatural is the greatest reality here and now." Eternity is here and now because God is here and now.

"Eternity breaks into time and gives it a real present," Tillich says. Sometimes it intrudes on the whole of history, as when God broke into human experience in sending Jesus. At other times, it comes as smaller breakthroughs, when we as individuals experience the presence of God. As Jesus said, "Now this is eternal life: that they may know you, the only true God, and Jesus Christ, whom you have sent" (John 17:3). When our knowledge of God is a present reality, so is our experience of eternity. And so is our experience of awe.

As Elizabeth Barrett Browning wrote,

> Earth's crammed with heaven,
> And every common bush afire with God,
> And only he who sees takes off his shoes,
> The rest sit around and pluck blackberries.

Practicing the Presence

We have all experienced timeless moments when we we're so occupied with something precious to us that we're totally unaware of the passing of time. Children often have such moments. Art is an attempt to recapture this childhood experience of arrested time—to freeze the past to be enjoyed later. As

Keats said, "A thing of beauty is a joy forever; Its loveliness increases; it will never pass into nothingness."

But of course it will. Art will last only as long as time does. The quick trip most books make from bookstore shelves to discount outlets makes us wonder if it lasts that long.

Art and absorption are not timeless. The only real timelessness is contact with God. In worship we transcend time and commune with the eternal. Prayer allows us to reach outside of time to our timeless God. Baptism is our participation in the death, burial, and resurrection of Jesus, from which we rise to a new life (Rom. 6:3–4). In the Lord's Supper, we receive his promise that "whoever eats my flesh and drinks my blood has eternal life" (John 6:54). All of us as his church have been raised "up with Christ and seated . . . with him in the heavenly realms" (Eph. 2:4–6).

So how can we become aware of the eternal, the holy, in our daily lives? By practicing the presence of God, cultivating our inner life with him, working to see God in nature, people, his Word, and our own hearts.

Dale Brown says that we "need the continual refreshment of a daily disciplined encounter with God. Only a continual remembering of our temporary state can motivate us to eternal action."

Devotional Thoughts on Time and Eternity

"This is the day the Lord has made;
let us rejoice and be glad in it."
—*Psalm 118:24*

Worry does not empty tomorrow of its sorrow, it empties today of its strength.

"Do not be anxious about anything, but in everything, by prayer and petition, with thanksgiving, present your requests to God. And the peace of God, which transcends all understanding, will guard your hearts and your minds in Christ Jesus."
—*Philippians 4:6–7*

In the presence
Of the world's pressures,

Preserve me
So that I might know
The stillness of Your peace.
    —*John M. Drescher*

"Be still, and know that I am God."
    —*Psalm 46:10*

A pure, sincere, and stable spirit is not distracted, though it be employed in many works; for it works all to the honor of God, and inwardly being still and quiet, seeks not itself in any thing it doth.
    —*Thomas à Kempis*

"For we are God's workmanship, created in Christ Jesus to do good works, which God prepared in advance for us to do."
    —*Ephesians 2:10*

God has created each one to do some definite service; he has committed some work to me which he has not committed to another. . . . Therefore I will trust him.
    —*John Henry Newman*

"Cast all your anxiety on him because he cares for you."
    —*1 Peter 5:7*

The time you now spend in prayer is always regained by what you save from worry and uncertainty. God has one Son who lived without sin, but he has no son who lived without prayer. Pray when you think you do not have time and when there seems to be no way; God specializes in the impossible.

"Pray continually."
    —*1 Thessalonians 5:17*

In the name of Jesus Christ, who was never in a hurry, we pray, O God, that thou wilt slow us down, for we know that we live too fast. With all of eternity before us, make us take time to live—time to get acquainted with thee, time to enjoy our blessings, and time to get to know each other.
    —*Peter Marshall*

"And we know that in all things God works for the good of those who love him, who have been called according to his purpose."
    —*Romans 8:28*

Forgive when I let
    The dust of the world's desires
Blur and blind my eyes
    So that I do not see
Thy guiding stars,

And the value of things invisible
And eternal.
                    —*John M. Drescher*

"Holy, holy, holy
is the Lord God Almighty,
who was, and is, and is to come."
                    —*Revelation 4:8*

"In the beginning, O Lord, you laid the foundations of
    the earth,
and the heavens are the work of your hands.
They will perish, but you remain."
                    —*Hebrews 1:10*

Lord, I do fear
Thou'st made the world too beautiful this year.
                    —*Edna St. Vincent Millay*

"Holy, holy, holy is the Lord Almighty; the whole earth is full of his glory."
                    —*Isaiah 6:1, 3*

Fill life
    With the fragrance of faith,,
The radiance of hope,
    And the sunlight of love,
Until all
    Is raised to newness of life
Through the living Christ.
                    —*John M. Drescher*

"The Lord is my strength and my song; he has become my salvation."
                    —*Exodus 15:2*

Cultivating the inner life demands solitude and silence. As Mother Teresa has said, "We need to find God, and he cannot be found in noise and restlessness. God is the friend of silence." Mother Teresa was not suggesting a monastic existence, since she herself lives in the thick of things, working among the teeming millions of India.

In this world of Muzak and chatter and crowded schedules, silence is hard to come by. And how can the mother of small children ever hope to find it? How can she, like Mary, ponder the events of her contact with God in her heart? (Luke 2:19).

Some women choose the early morning hours, before anyone else is awake. Some stay up late at night. Some use their children's naptime. One friend of mine retreats to the bathroom to find a little time alone with God.

Devotional literature can be an aid to centering our minds on God. Such classics of religious thought as Pascal, à Kempis, and Merton can lift our hearts above the mundane to God's very presence. More popular devotional works, such as Oswald Chambers' *My Utmost for His Highest*, Mrs. Charles E. Cowman's *Streams in the Desert*, and Hannah Whitehall Smith's *The Christian's Secret of a Happy Life*, are also helpful.

Journal-keeping is another useful technique. Gordon Mac-Donald suggests entering an account of the things you've accomplished, the people you've encountered, the things you've learned, the feelings and impressions you've experienced. He also writes prayers, insights, and concerns in his journal. He keeps his journal from front to back of a bound notebook. Then from back to front he keeps his prayer list and excerpts from his daily reading. When the two ends meet, he gets another notebook.

Down from the Mountain

Experiencing the presence of God in personal devotions is a mountaintop event, but we can't live there. Moses, after receiving the law from the hand of God on Mount Sinai, had to go down again and confront the sin of the Israelites. Even Jesus, after his Transfiguration, descended to deal with sickness and a lack of faith. We, too, must come down from the mountain to confront the realities of life.

Anthropologist Joseph Campbell, in an interview with Bill Moyers, spoke of how much he enjoyed visiting St. Patrick's Cathedral. Located in the middle of the economic center of New York City, it gave him a wonderful sense of God's presence when he walked in, and a burning desire to take some of the experience with him when he walked back out into the world.

That should be our desire as we worship God, both as a body and as individuals. Life is temporary. The mountain is our true home. But we live both in time, subject to sin and death, and in Christ, being made righteous and alive.

As William H. Davis puts it, "The best preparation for living well *then* is learning to live well *now*." But someone has said, "Millions of people hope to live forever who do not know what to do with themselves on a rainy Sunday afternoon." Davis suggests that "each day . . . be viewed as a sort of miniature eternity. Each day can be filled with excellent things—a kind word to this person, a surprise visit or letter to that, some job well done, even though it might be a small, routine chore. Each day can be lived 'as unto the Lord,' basking in his presence, talking and walking hand in hand with Jesus."

When we live this way—practicing the presence of God both on the mountaintop and in the valley with its practical demands—eternity will be our common state, and the transition at the end of our lives will be natural and easy.

As Fulton J. Sheen wrote, each moment of our lives affects eternity:

> Every moment comes to you
>   pregnant with a divine
> purpose; time being so

precious that God deals
it out only second by
second. Once it leaves
your hands and your power
to do with it as you
please, it plunges into
eternity, to remain forever
what you made it.

Questions and Activities

1. Name the events in your life that have made death more real and personal to you. Have they led you

to repent?

to live a more distinctive lifestyle?

to appreciate life more?

to serve?

2. Paul tells us that "though outwardly we are wasting away, yet inwardly we are being renewed day by day." List three ways your inner woman is being renewed.

3. Since memorizing Scripture is a great asset in thinking God's thoughts, list the verses you know by heart and the Scriptures you would like to memorize.

4. The devotional book I plan to read in the next year is:

5. Even though the clock is ticking, step out of time for a few moments to contact the eternal right now with some special thought of praise and awe.

Now come down from the mountain to touch one special person with the beauty and strength God has provided.

BIBLIOGRAPHY

Abrams, Mary. "Seize the Moment—It's Yours!" *Graduate Woman* (September/October 1979).

Banks, Robert. *The Tyranny of Time: When 24 Hours Is Not Enough.* Downers Grove, Ill.: InterVarsity Press, 1983.

Barnett, Chris. "Workaholics: They're Not All Work Enthusiasts." *Republic Scene* (January 1982).

Barnett, Joe R. *Making the Most of Time: A Four-Step Program for Effective Time Management.* Lubbock: Pathway Evangelism, 1980.

Berges, Marshall. "The Ray Bradburys." *Los Angeles Times Home Magazine* (January 27, 1974).

Blanchard, Kenneth and Spencer Johnson. *The One Minute Manager.* New York: William Morrow and Company, 1982.

Boorstin, Daniel J. *The Discoverers: A History of Man's Search to Know His World and Himself.* New York: Vintage Books, 1985.

Campolo, Tony. *The Success Fantasy.* Wheaton, Ill.: Victor, 1980.

Clayton, John. "The Bible's Unique Concept of Time." *Does God Exist?* (no. 1, 10).

Colson, Charles. "Life and Death." *The Saturday Evening Post* (January/February 1984).

Congo, David and Janet. *Less Stress: The 10-Minute Stress Reduction Plan.* Ventura, Calif.: Regal, 1985.

Connolly, Patrick. "Time Management." *The Sunday Tennessean* (April 3, 1988).

Conrad, Barnaby. "My Four Weeks at the Betty Ford Center." *Los Angeles Times Magazine* (January 11, 1987).

Cormack, David. *Fighting for Time: Fifteen Rounds in the Fight for Effective Use of Time.* Old Tappan, N.J.: Revell, 1986.

Culp, Stephanie. *How to Get Organized When You Don't Have the Time.* Cincinnati: Writer's Digest Books, 1986.

Cumberti, Betty. "Challenge to Working Mothers." *Los Angeles Times* (June 22, 1987).

Daniels, Shirley and Marian Jones Clark. *Managing to Be Free: A Practical Guide to Organizing Home Priorities.* Grand Rapids: Baker, 1987.

Davis, William H. "Transcending Time." *20th Century Christian* (March 1980).

Dobson, James. *What Wives Wish Their Husbands Knew about Women.* Wheaton: Tyndale House, 1975.

Doheny, Kathleen. "Making Time for Exercise to Fit Your Goals." *Los Angeles Times* 30, (March 1988).

Douglass, Stephen B. "How to Beat the Clock." *Moody Monthly* (April 1979).

Engstrom, Ted W. and R. Alec McKenzie. *Managing Your Time: Practical Guidelines on the Effective Use of Time.* Grand Rapids: Zondervan, 1988.

Fleming, Jane. "When Busy Is Too Busy." *Christianity Today* (April 22, 1988).

Foster, Richard. "Is This the Year to Get Organized?" *Christian Herald* (January 1988).

Galloway, Dale E. *Dare to Discipline Yourself.* Old Tappan, N.J.: Revell, 1984.

Gardner, Neely. "The Effective Use of the Manager's Time." *News Notes of California Libraries* 64 (Spring 1969).

Gibbs, Nancy. "How America Has Run Out of Time." *Time* (April 24, 1989).

Girdwood, Phyllis. "Growing the Gift of Hospitality." *The Lookout* (May 24, 1987).

Glass, Esther Eby. "Stewardship of Time." *A Farthing in Her Hand: Stewardship for Women.* Edited by Helen Alderfee. Scottdale, Pa.: Herald Press, 1964.

Goodman, Ellen. "Solution to the Time Crunch." *Los Angeles Times* (August 30, 1988).

Growald, Eileen Rockefeller and Allan Leeks. "Beyond Self." *American Health* (March 1988).

Hobbs, Charles R. *Time Power.* New York: Harper & Row, 1987.

Hummel, C.E. *Tyranny of the Urgent.* Madison: InterVarsity Press, 1967.

"I'll Do It . . . Tomorrow: Breaking the Procrastination Habit." *Christopher News Notes* (June/July 1986).

"It's about Time." *Christopher News Notes* (January/February 1978).

Jones, Milton. "How's Your Quiet Time?" *Campus Journal* (Winter 1984).

Kane, Carolyn. "Thinking: A Neglected Art." *Newsweek* (December 14, 1981).

Knaus, William J. *Do It Now: How to Stop Procrastinating.* Englewood Cliffs, N.J.: Prentice-Hall, 1979.

Lakein, Alan. *How to Get Control of Your Time and Your Life.* New York: Signet, 1973.

___. "How to Use Your Time Wisely." *U.S. News and World Report* (January 19, 1976).

LeBoeuf, Michael. *Working Smart: How to Accomplish More in Half the Time.* New York: Warner, 1979.

Lee, Mary Dean. "The Great Balancing Act." *Psychology Today* (March 1986).

Levine, Robert. "Social Time: The Heartbeat of Culture." *Psychology Today* (March 1985).

Lindsey, Nancy Mitchum. "A Realistic Perspective: Possible Problems and Critical Choices for Aged Christians and Their Families." *Mission Journal* (September 1982).

"A Little at a Time." *A Magazet* (April 1963).

Mains, Karen. *Making Sunday Special*. Waco, Tex.: Word, 1987.

MacDonald, Gordon. *Ordering Your Private World*. Nashville: Nelson, 1985.

———. *Restoring Your Spiritual Passion*. Nashville: Oliver Nelson, 1986.

Mackenzie, R. Alec. *The Time Trap: How to Get More Done in Less Time*. New York: McGraw-Hill, 1972.

MacNeil/Lehrer NewsHour. "Functional Illiteracy." Public Broadcasting System (May 23, 1988).

McConnell, William T. *The Gift of Time*. Downers Grove, Ill.: InterVarsity Press, 1983.

Miller, Judy. *Seasons of Celebration*. Pasadena, Tex.: Dawn Publications, 1987.

Moosbrugger, Ed. "Theft of Time." *Evening Outlook* (January 20, 1977).

Naisbitt, John. *Megatrends*. New York: Warner, 1982.

Neff, David. "Have I Done Well?" *Christianity Today* (February 17, 1989).

Olbricht, Thomas H. *The Power to Be: The Life-Style of Jesus from Mark's Gospel*. Austin, Tex.: Journey Books, 1979.

Oldenburg, Don. "Time Compression: It's Gaining on Us." *Los Angeles Times* (September 24, 1987).

O'Reilly, Jane. "How to Get Control of Your Time." *The Art of Living*. New York: Berkley Books, 1980.

Ortlund, Anne. *Disciplines of the Beautiful Woman*. Waco, Tex.: Word, 1977.

Otto, Donna. *All in Good Time*. Nashville: Nelson, 1985.

Sanders, J. Oswald. "The Christian's Problem of Time." *Moody Monthly* (May 1967).

Schantz, Daniel. "Whittle Your Work Down to Size." *The Lookout* (February 21, 1988).

Schlack, Janis. "There's Nothing You Can Do?" *The Lookout* (September 6, 1987).

Scott, Dru. *How to Put More Time in Your Life*. New York: Signet, 1980.

Shedd, Charlie. *Time for All Things*. Nashville: Abingdon, 1962.

Sheehy, Gail, *Passages: Predictable Crises of Adult Life*. New York: E.P. Dutton, 1976.

Stacey, Julie. "What We Think about Work." *USA Today* (June 1987).

Stein, George. "Widow Earns College Degree after 49 Years." *Los Angeles Times* (August 7, 1987).

Swindoll, Charles R. *Growing Strong in the Seasons of Life.* Portland, Ore.: Multnomah Press, 1983.

Tavris, Carol. "Anger Defused." *Psychology Today* (November 1982).

Taylor, Harold J. *Making Time Work for You: A Guide Book for Effective and Productive Time Management.* New York: Beaufort Books.

Taylor, Lesley. "Americans Volunteer Poll Shows." *Evening Outlook* (October 26, 1988).

Teel, Gordon. "Taking Time to Live." *20th Century Christian* (December 1979).

"The 10 Happiest Things You Can Do." *Prevention Magazine* (December 1983).

Tillich, Paul. *The Shaking of the Foundation.* London: Penguin Books, 1949.

Timm, Paul R. *Successful Self-Management: A Psychologically Sound Approach to Personal Effectiveness.* Los Altos, Calif.: Crisp Publications, 1987.

"Today." *Christopher News Notes* (June/July 1983).

Tournier, Paul. *The Adventure of Living.* New York: Harper & Row, 1965.

___. *Learn To Grow Old.* New York: Harper & Row, 1972.

___. *The Seasons of Life.* Atlanta: John Knox Press, 1963.

Turla, Peter and Kathleen L. Hawkins. *Time Management Made Easy.* New York: E. P. Dutton, 1983.

Ures, Auren and Jane Bensahel. "Bits of 'Waste Time' Add Up Usefully." *Los Angeles Times* (February 22, 1980).

"What Are You Doing with Your Life?" *Christopher News Notes* (May 1973).

Winston, Stephanie. *Getting Organized.* New York: Warner Books, 1978.

Yancey, Philip. "Art or Chernobyl: Which Matters More?" *Christianity Today* (September 16, 1988).

"ZZZZZ-Z-Z-Z." *Los Angeles Times* (May 1985).

INDEX